DOUBLE MISSION

DOUBLE MISSION

RAF Fighter Ace and SOE Agent

Manfred Czernin, DSO, MC, DFC

Norman L. R. Franks

WILLIAM KIMBER · LONDON

First published in 1976 by
WILLIAM KIMBER & CO. LIMITED
Godolphin House, 22a Queen Anne's Gate,
London, SW1H 9AE

ISBN 0 7183 0254 0

Typeset by
Specialised Offset Services, Liverpool
and printed in Great Britain by
The Pitman Press, Bath.

It is required of a man that he should share the passion and action of his time, at peril of being judged not to have lived.

OLIVER WENDELL HOLMES (1809-1894)
Justice of the United States Supreme Court

Contents

List of Illustrations

MAPS IN THE TEXT

Acknowledgments

No biography can be written without considerable help. I am, therefore, indebted to many people who gave their time to meet or to correspond with me.

To Manfred's mother, The Hon. Mrs Lucile Frost, to Countess Maud Czernin, and to Manfred's daughter Carolyn and son Nicholas I am most grateful for their help and forbearance.

For recollections of his early life I must say thank you to Mr Laurence Shaw, Dr C. Skelton-Smalley, Dr D. I. Crowther and Mr Hugh A. F. Latimer.

To the men of the Royal Air Force who flew with him or knew him in the service I am also grateful. Marshal of the RAF Sir Dermot Boyle GCB KCVO KBE AFC, Air Vice Marshal Richard C. Ayling CB CBE MBIM, Air Vice Marshal Neil Cameron CBE DSO DFC, Air Commodore Harold A. C. Bird-Wilson CBE DSO DFC AFC, Group Captain David J. Alvey OBE, Group Captain Peter Townsend CVO DSO DFC, Group Captain Leonard S. Snaith CB AFC, Group Captain Denis Lyster DSO DFC AFC, Group Captain J. O. W. Oliver CB DSO DFC, Group Captain Leonard H. Bartlett DSO, Group Captain J. A. Hemingway DFC, Wing Commander F. M. Smith DFC, Squadron Leader Desmond Fopp AFC, Glyn Griffiths DFM, and to Ministry of Defence, department AR8b (RAF).

For background to the air war I am particularly grateful to Mr Peter Cornwell for his deep researches into the Battle of Britain, especially from the German side, also Herr Hans Ring and of course to General Adolf Galland. Assistance with the RAF chapters was also given by my friends Chaz Bowyer and Christopher F. Shores, and also Mr Ian McLachlan.

Special thanks are also due to the men of Special Operations. General Sir Colin Gubbins, KCMG, DSO, MC, Lieutenant Colonel Richard T. Hewitt, OBE, MA, Major Tom Rowarth, DSO, Major Gordon Lett, DSO, Major Richard Tolson, Mr C. H. Brock and Giuliano Mattioli, and also Mario Invernicci.

Manfred's friends too must be thanked. Mr & Mrs Pat Ricard, Mr & Mrs Alwyn Bolton and Walter Parslow. Mr G. Boella of Fiats and also Dr Gavin Thurston also have my thanks.

Lastly but not least, to my wife Kate for putting up with my incessant typing and for correcting and proof reading the manuscript.

CHAPTER ONE

A Man is Born

January 1913 in the German capital of Berlin seemed little different from any previous January. As always it was cold. Snow was in the air and only those people who needed to be out of their homes, left the warmth of their firesides. To at least one person, however, winter's icy fingers had no chilling effect. The Countess Lucile Czernin had just given birth to her fourth son.

Lucile Czernin was the wife of Count Otto Czernin von and Zu Chudenitz of Dimokur, Austria, who was in his country's diplomatic service. His chosen profession had taken him to many parts of Europe and the early 1900s found him at the Austrian Embassy in Rome. Attending a ball in that great and ancient city, he met the woman who was to become his wife, the young, attractive Lucy (Lucile) Katharine Beckett, the daughter of Ernest William Beckett, 2nd Baron Grimthorpe. At this time she was living with her grandmother in Rome, where she was having a preliminary 'coming out' before being officially presented in London. The friendship of the Austrian diplomat and the English debutante which followed soon blossomed into something more but the courtship had to be delayed till she had at least completed part of the 'season' in London. Following this, they were eventually married in London on July 27, 1903, shortly after her nineteenth birthday.

The first years of their marriage proved happy and they were soon blessed with three sons, Paul, Jaromir, and Edmund, all fine, healthy boys. In 1909 Otto was sent to Roumania, but two and a half years later, prior to the birth of their fourth child, he was ordered to St Petersburg (later known as Petrograd) in Russia. While they had lived in Roumania, Lucile had had a friendly association with Crown Princess Maria who had been looking forward with interest to the arrival of the Czernin's new baby. With the sudden news of his transfer, Otto decided to proceed to St Petersburg alone, where he would have time to set up home for his family, while Lucile travelled to Berlin, for it was agreed that the severe Russian winter should be avoided. Lucile, therefore, stayed at a small hotel in Berlin until the child arrived. This arrangement proved more than suitable for her sister was in a Berlin clinic, having been there some while, so she was able to spend some time with her during her stay. On the eighteenth day of the new year of 1913, her fourth son was born.

The news of the child's arrival soon reached the Crown Princess and needless to say it was a great honour when the Princess suggested being his godmother at the forthcoming Christening.

Lucile, meantime, had decided that the boy's name would be Manfred, a personal choice taken from her own hero from history, King Manfred, of Sicily. When, as a young girl she had first visited the beautiful family villa at Ravello, overlooking the Bay of Salerno, she was not only captivated by the villa but with the history of the surrounding country. Reading avidly the history of Southern Italy and of Sicily, she had met in the pages of many books this son of the Emperor Frederick III, who had lived between 1232 and 1266 AD. That Manfred had been a gallant king, acting loyally and with vigour in the execution of his duties. On a rumour in 1258 that Conradin was dead, Manfred was crowned King of Sicily and Palermo in August of that year. That rumour proved to be false but the new king declined to abdicate, pointing out the necessity for a strong native ruler, rather than King Conradin. In company with Ghibellines, he defeated Guelphs at Monte Alperto in 1260 but was eventually defeated and killed near Benevento in 1266.

This, then, was how Manfred Czernin acquired his name, a name which means 'Man of Peace'. In retrospect, a strange name for a man who would be anything but a man of peace in a war as yet undreamed of.

When Manfred was born, Princess Maria was herself with child, and she and Lucile had on one occasion been discussing what name would be chosen for the baby. Otto wanted, if it should prove to be another son, the name Frederick, after a brother of his who had recently died, but Lucile, in answer to the Princess's question, had quickly said,

'If it's a boy, I want to call him Manfred.'

Princess Maria was delighted. If she had been free to name her own children, she confided, Manfred would be a name she would like to choose. Otto's choice was therefore over-ridden and Manfred it came to be.

When the young child was about six weeks old, the family went to Monte Carlo, where the Count went every year to compete in the clay-pigeon shooting tournament. Then, in April, they returned to the family's new home in Russia. In June the Countess went to Finland with her sons where she spent the summer, the Count spending week-ends with them whenever possible.

This happy time was, unfortunately, coming to an end. Relations between Otto and Lucile became strained and in March 1914 they agreed upon a separation. The Count took custody of the three older boys, who were now at school, while Lucile kept the young baby, but on the understanding that he would join his father following his seventh birthday. So it was that Lucile Czernin again found herself at her grandmother's house in Rome, this time with her youngest son. In June she took Manfred to her father's villa Cimbrone at Ravello, and it was here that Manfred was to spend his holidays in later life.

With the coming of summer, the distant dark clouds of war were beginning to cast their terrible shadows across the continent of Europe. Following the assassination of the Austrian Archduke Ferdinand, the world was suddenly confronted with the beginning of the most terrible war in history. For four long years the allied nations of Britain, France, Belgium, Italy – and later America – were locked in mortal combat with Germany and its ally, the Austro-Hungarian Empire.

Lucile and Manfred spent the whole of the First World War in Italy. Her grandmother was taken ill in 1915 and as Lucile was still an Austrian subject by marriage when the old lady died, she was unable to acquire a British passport. Being officially termed an 'enemy alien' in spite of being British by birth, she was not allowed to move out of the country. It had been fortunate that she had spent so much of her life in Rome with her grandmother and had become well-known. In addition, she was fortunate in being a friend of the British Ambassador, Sir Rennell Rodd, so she was accepted as being under the protection of the British Embassy. So for the remainder of the war, she busied herself in war relief work.

On occasions the situation proved an embarrassment. One day in 1917 when Manfred was four years old, his Nanny went into the Central Post Office in Rome while she was out walking with him. As

Nanny stood waiting in a queue, Manfred suddenly looked up at her and asked in a high-pitched voice:

'Is is true, Nanny, that I am an Austrian?' All the people drew to one side and looked horror-stricken at this potential enemy of Italy. Poor Nanny seized her young charge and beat a hasty retreat. It was never discovered how he had found out about his nationality at this young age.

Manfred soon developed an adventuresome attitude to life. One day, at about the same time as the Post Office episode, his Nanny was sitting in a nearby park whilst he played happily about her. All at once she happened to glance up just in time to see him about to heave a large rock he had picked up into a nearby baby carriage. Just in time she managed to prevent him harming the small child inside.

On another occasion during the war, the Ambassador's wife, Lady Rodd, organised a performance of *A Midsummer Night's Dream*, at the Embassy, to be enacted by local children between the ages of 12 and 16. It was in the aid of a war charity and the smaller children who also attended, were seated on the floor in front of the stage. His mother placed young Manfred among the rest of the children, and then wondered if she should stay nearby where he could see her and perhaps be better behaved, or move to the rear of the room. She decided on the latter, hoping that her absence might make him sit still. To her horror she suddenly saw her small, blue-clad son, climbing up onto the stage. Fortunately Lady Rodd reached him in time and pulled him back by the seat of his pants. Some years later the Countess met an Italian lady who had been one of the group of small children. Manfred had, she related, been the hero in all of the children's eyes, and in the same instant, the horror of all the mothers and nannies present.

Manfred developed an early affection for animals of every kind, and there seemed to exist a natural and mutual affinity and love between them. This association with animals got off to an inauspicious start when, at about the age of three, his nanny found him trying to stuff a kitten into a water jug. Some three years after this episode, his mother went to visit friends at their country villa just outside Rome, taking Manfred with her. These friends had an enormous white Roman sheep-dog, employed as a very effective guard dog. It was kept chained up at the front door during the day and was considered very ferocious. After lunching, the Countess sent Manfred out into the rear garden to play, and about an hour later, she and her hosts stepped out onto the balcony to call him in. When they could not see him, they went round to the front of the house and when they saw him, there was some slight panic, for Manfred was lying between the front paws of this large animal with his arms clasped about its neck, apparently the best of friends. As a boy and later when a man, he could rarely pass a dog in the street without patting and talking to it. Throughout his childhood and later youth in England, he slept with his two alsatians, Noel and Stella, on his bed whenever he was at home. During his holidays they were inseparable companions. In Italy his dog had been Leo, a beautiful, powerful Great Dane.

When peace came to the world in 1918, young Manfred was nearing his sixth birthday, but had not been affected by the war that had ravaged not only the fields and towns of France and Belgium but also the northern provinces of Italy. Having spent his days in Rome, and at Ravello during the hot Italian summers, he had grown into a happy, lively and energetic child who always seemed to be in some form of mischief or adventure.

One would have imagined that with only one of her four sons with her, Countess Czernin would have been a very protective mother; in fact she tried to be the opposite. She firmly believed that children who were constantly cautioned and frightened of the dangers that surrounded them, grew up with more fear of these things than was necessary. It was probably this attitude in his upbringing that made Manfred the fearless man he was to become in his adult life, for no danger or difficult situation was to prove too great for him.

As an illustration of this attitude, one day his mother found him, while he was still a very small boy, climbing a large tree. At any moment, she thought, he could slip and fall but realised that if she called out it might scare him, so without a word, she turned and walked away. Manfred of course, returned to the ground, the conqueror of the tree and without injury. He soon became independent as well. On his seventh birthday his mother bought him a bicycle and at once he wanted to ride it. She took him from the house in the Trinita du Monti, onto a broad sidewalk that led to the Pincio Gardens. Enrico, the Countess's chauffeur, helped him to mount the machine but from that moment he would not entertain any further help or assistance, determined to master the bike on his own. A few minutes later he and his mother met a friend and he dutifully dismounted to greet her. They began to walk towards the park and the friend offered to help him back onto the saddle but no, he would do it himself, and soon he developed the art of remaining upright without help.

It was now 1920 and as Manfred was seven years old, the Countess, true to her promise, wrote to her former husband Otto, prepared, as much as any mother in her position could be prepared, to return her son to his father as agreed.

Otto had left the diplomatic service to join the Austrian Army with whom he served during the last two years of the war. When the Austrian and Hungarian Alliance broke up, he returned to his mother's home in Bohemia – Czechoslovakia as it now is. His brother, Graff Ottokar Czernin, Manfred's uncle, had been the Austrian Foreign Minister during the latter war years. In fact in January 1917, he and the Chef de Cabinet, Count Hoyos, had visited Berlin and, at a luncheon, the Order of the Black Eagle had been conferred on Ottokar by the German Emperor. Others present at that luncheon had been Herr Simmermann, the German Minister for Foreign Affairs, Herr von Bethmann, Hollwegg and Field Marshal von Hindenburg. Now, however, the war was over, and it had been lost.

There was an anxious period of waiting for Otto's reply, and, when it came, relief and happiness flooded through the Countess. She could keep the boy! It would be far better, Otto wrote, for Manfred to grow up and be educated in a great country than in the miserable remains of defeated Austria. There could be alas, no reconciliation between himself and Lucile; she made it clear that she would not return to Otto, thereby abandoning for the moment her other three sons and causing a rift between the two surviving boys and Manfred which was never to heal. Their separation had become official in October 1914, and in 1920 they completed divorce proceedings. The overriding factor throughout this trying time was that she had her young son. Manfred was hers for ever! Whatever else she had lost, that small bundle of adventuresome, mischievous energy was hers. The fears of him being taken from her were now passed and that one agonising thought that one day he would be no longer with her was finally dispelled. It was now Manfred and her, she must plan, prepare, and guide him through life as she had loved and taught him from the moment of his birth.

CHAPTER TWO

From Youth to Manhood

Manfred's mother's first decision was of education for her son. She eventually decided that her native England should be the place to go. This was influenced to some extent, in that she could find no governess in Italy able to cope adequately with him. She therefore travelled to England that spring, and taking advice from her brother, sent Manfred to a Dame School in Folkestone administered by a Mrs Hylton. He joined this lady in May 1920, staying there until the Countess could make further arrangements for him to be sent to a suitable school.

Meantime, she returned to Italy where she continued with her social work. Then, during the school holidays, tragedy struck the Czernin family. Going to Florence, the Countess met her three eldest boys from school, planning to take them down to Ravello for a holiday.

In Italy at that time there was a great deal of political unrest between the Communist and Fascist elements and suddenly, by sheer bad luck, the Czernin motor car drove into one of the trouble spots. Lucile Czernin took a turn in driving the car, sitting next to her was the eldest son Paul who was now 17. Edmund, 16, and Jaromir, 15, sat in the back with Enrico, her chauffeur.

As they approached Viterbo, the town in which they had planned to stay overnight, they were stopped at the city gates by a group of Communists under the command of an officer. The officer refused to allow the car into the city, the Countess was informed that she would have to drive around the town and continue on her way. The hotel at which the family were to have stayed was only just inside the gates, but the officer was adamant, therefore she had no alternative but to turn and depart. No sooner had she gathered speed than, from the city wall and from a nearby ditch or trench, all hell broke loose. The Communist forces simply opened fire at practically point-blank-range, sending a hail of bullets into the car. The Countess put her foot down on the throttle, trying desperately to get away from the firing, and looking for a road that might lead them away from the town. From the rear of the car, Enrico was yelling at her to stop, and seeing a churchyard ahead, she drove the car alongside one of the high walls for some measure of protection. Slamming on the brakes she turned her head to see her son Jaromir lying dead with a bullet wound in the head. Enrico had also been hit by a burst from a shot-gun which had sent pellets into the back of his head and neck. The Countess leapt from the car, shouting at the top of her voice for the men to stop shooting.

'You have killed my son, you have killed my son,' she cried out.

The firing ceased and the officer was running towards her. Paul tried to get out of the car but his left leg crumpled and he fell to the ground. He had been hit in the knee, the bullet having passed right through the joint before hitting the floor only an inch or two from his mother's foot. He was losing blood rapidly, and Enrico was also in a bad way. The officer and some of his men helped them into the town and into the very hotel at which they had hoped to stay, and towards which, only a few short minutes before, they had been peacefully driving.

Paul was seriously ill, his face beginning to turn black with the loss of blood. It was essential for him to have immediate help as his leg had been practically severed. The leg was in fact amputated, but he was to suffer from his injury for the rest of his life. Enrico went down with tetanus, his wounds having become infected, but at least he, like Paul, had survived.

The Communist troops had, they later admitted, thought the family was a party of fascists making off from the town gates, for parties of fascists had been known to have been driven about by women to allay suspicion. If only the officer had let them pass into the hotel, he could have questioned them at his leisure.

When she had recovered from her grief, if a mother can ever fully recover from the tragic death of a son, Countess Czernin returned to England to arrange for Manfred's schooling.

Following many enquiries, it was found to be too late to put Manfred's name down for Eton, but a friend, Hubert Beaumont, had a son at Oundle School, near Peterborough. As he warmly recommended the school, she applied at once, Manfred being accepted without further question. It was now 1923, and Manfred was ten years old.

The history of Oundle School dates back to 1485 when it was originally a Guild School. Over the years it gradually grew in size and popularity, its buildings extended and constantly added to until it dominated the small town of Oundle. Manfred's first headmaster was Dr K. Fisher, who had taken over from the distinguished Dr Sanderson in 1922.

Manfred joined the Berrystead (Junior House), remaining there until 1927. He had no liking for his early prep days and made no bones about it. The smaller boys were always dominated by the older youths in the public school but when later he joined the older pupils, life took on a rosier hue. His mother, meantime, had taken a house in Princes Risborough in Buckinghamshire, continuing to devote herself to social work, mainly in the East End of London.

These early school days for Manfred were made more tolerable by the summer holidays when his mother, who changed her name by Deed Poll in July 1922 to Mrs Beckett (her maiden name), took him back each year to Ravello. He was still more than a little adventuresome and playful; one incident seeming to be typical of his forming character. Shortly before they came to England, they visited Capri and the Countess left Manfred playing while going out from the beach in a rowing boat. She was some distance from the shore and he was happily playing on the sand. Nearby stood some very high-diving boards and these suddenly took his attention. Within a few minutes he had climbed onto the top board and seemed at any moment about to jump into the sea below. His mother spotted him and quickly began to row towards the boards. At this time, he could not swim but this small detail was not going to be allowed to come between him and his desire to leap into the sea. Before his mother reached the spot, Manfred jumped, happily splashing about and treading water until his anxious mother was near enough to fish him out.

As the years passed, and Manfred grew into a young man, school became more acceptable, but only as a means to an end. There were about 580 boys at the school, and he soon began to stand out among his immediate circle of friends. He was a cheerful boy, easy to get along with but with a penchant for getting into minor scrapes. Indeed, as one of his friends recalled '... if anyone seemed most likely to be expelled it would be him.' He is remembered as being a very colourful person, also an individual – a well-loved nonconformist, who was both kind and gentle. It was this somewhat independent characteristic that endeared him to his friends and fellow school chums. Because of this quality he was most popular, but of course the masters had other views.

The boys at Oundle were required to work in the school workshops for a week on occasion as part of the curriculum. One day they were at work with a large seven foot long lathe, which had a three to five inch swing. Manfred somehow caught his left arm in the overhead belt and before he could even think to get clear his arm was pulled down and caught in the drum. He gave a short cry of pain but then made no further fuss or even complained while he was being freed, although it must have been a painful experience. For the next few days, however, he was quite the hero with his bandaged arm hanging in a sling.

His work on the academic side was not very brilliant, he probably did just enough work to get by, but went no further. He must have eventually improved slightly and shown his intelligent side, for he finished in the Classical Vth Form, in which the school had most of its real scholars. In 1927 he left the Junior House, moving to Bramston House where he stayed for one year before moving again to a new House that had just been opened. Apart from his studies he developed a sincere love of good music, sang in the school choir, as well as playing the violin in the school orchestra, taking part in the annual oratorios, notably Handel's Messiah and Bach's Mass in B Minor. This awoke in Manfred a love of music which was to become one of his chief joys throughout his life, and Oundle initiated him in some of the greatest music in the world.

He developed an interest, rather than excelling in, sport, taking part in rowing, cricket, (a love of the latter remained with him) and he eventually joined the MCC in the late 1930s. To those not closely associated with him, he seemed to be a quiet lad who kept to himself, but the friends he made knew him to be a loyal and reliable comrade. They all knew of course, that he was a count, although a mystery was perpetuated around him by his being always referred to as plain M. B. Czernin. He never boasted or traded on this openly, but one suspects that knowing that the other boys knew, or thought they knew, something of this title, was sufficient to create some sort of aura about him. When, from time to time he was referred to as the 'Count', it was usually in fun with no malice intended. To his teachers he appeared quite a normal youth, not seemingly particularly Austrian in any way, for his English was perfect with no Austrian or Italian accents. One of his teachers, Mr Laurence 'Tub' Shaw, remembers how normal he was, considering his rather difficult background.

Another thing Oundle taught him was military discipline, for the school had its own Officers' Training Corps which Manfred attended between 1928 to 1930.

One small incident that occurred during this period was later to be recalled by his mother. During half-terms she always took him out for trips in the country, especially to Cambridge, Ely and Peterborough. One afternoon they came to a very old little church, with some equally old tombstones. Returning to the car Manfred, looking very thoughtful, turned to his mother and said:

'I hope I die before you, Mum.' As events were to prove, he did.

His mother re-married in June 1926, her new husband being Captain Oliver Henry Frost, OBE, MC, who had been a pilot in the Royal Flying Corps and the Royal Air Force during the First World War, following service with the Middlesex Regiment. Manfred got on very well with Oliver and he was very happy about the marriage. They lived in a very nice house in York Terrace, by Regent's Park, where Manfred would spend his holidays when he did not go to Italy and to Ravello. A school friend once met Manfred in London soon after they had both left Oundle School, Manfred asking him to come home with him. This was quite in keeping with the way Manfred would so easily show his great friendship and the old school chum was very impressed with the 'most civilized house.' The lasting memory this young friend took with him was of an enormous gramophone which was, at that time, the last word in musical reproduction. It had a superb hand-made wooden horn which must have been at least seven foot long and four or five feet across at its mouth.

In 1930, Manfred asked his parents to let him leave Oundle without taking his school certificates, feeling that he had had more than enough of schooling. They reluctantly agreed, and so Manfred left Oundle but took with him many happy childhood memories.

The school had flourished and grown during his period there. During the period 1922 to 1945, 145 of its students went to Oxford or Cambridge Universities. One of Manfred's fellow students had been Joseph Simpson, who in 1924 had won the Recruits Shooting Cup and later in 1928 won the Lady Lyveden Athletics Cup. Simpson eventually became Head of House and after leaving Oundle went into the police force, becoming Sir Joseph. He died in 1968 as Chief Superintendent of the Metropolitan Police. Another scholar who was to gain fame was Peter Scott, the now well-known naturalist.

In the summer of 1930, the problem was, what should Manfred do to occupy his very active mind and body. He was now seventeen, tall and slim with light coloured hair brushed back. He had a theory that it was important for a man to have his hair recently cut but never should it look as if it had just been done!

His step-father arranged for him to go into an engineering firm where he was employed for about a year. Then a question arose about the possibilities of going to university. This would have entailed coaching for a further year so as to pass an entrance examination, but as neither his mother or Oliver thought he would settle down to doing much work at university, but would probably just have a good time, they decided it would be better for him to go out to one of the colonies, which he became eager to do.

Again it was a friend of Mrs Frost who helped to solve the problem. The famous author and friend of the Frosts, Francis Brett-Young, knew a Colonel Valentine who owned a large tobacco plantation in Southern Rhodesia. He agreed to write to Valentine to ask if he would be prepared to take Manfred as a sort of apprentice. As the Colonel was known to have three sons, all about Manfred's own age, it seemed an excellent plan.

While awaiting the reply Manfred was, one day, walking along Harley Street, and, passing the house of a friend, suddenly decided to drop in and see him. Welcomed inside, Manfred was introduced briefly to three or four young men seated about, all discussing their various plans for the future. Manfred was asked in turn what his immediate intentions were.

'Oh, I am going to Southern Rhodesia,' he replied brightly.

'Whereabouts in Rhodesia are you going?' asked one of the young men who was not known to him.

'To Umtali,' answered Manfred. The other asked with interest:

'And what do you plan to do there'. With his usual self-assurance Manfred replied without hesitation.

'I'm going to work on Colonel Valentine's plantation.' The other young man looked at Manfred for a moment, smiled, then said,

'I'm Valentine.'

Manfred was rather taken aback, for this man he then discovered was Sandy Valentine, the Colonel's eldest son. Fortunately Sandy and Manfred became great friends and in September Manfred left for Umtali.

When Mrs Frost visited the plantation on one occasion shortly afterwards, Colonel Valentine confided to her that he had decided at first not to take Manfred, for he had not had much success with so-called apprentices, but Sandy, having already met Manfred, persuaded his Father to let him come. This incident is typical of how many things came Manfred's way by a strange kind of fate, all his life.

Manfred spent two very happy years on the plantation and was taught a great deal about business management. Being thrust so close to nature in Rhodesia his natural love of animals flourished and he enjoyed tending and working with the domestic animals and seeing the African wild-life that abounded nearby. On the plantation, Colonel Valentine owned a horse who would allow no one to ride him. The Colonel had decided to have the animal destroyed, when Manfred asked if he could try to break the horse. With Manfred, the animal became as gentle as a lamb. Some months later this same horse tore its leg on some barbed wire, the leg having to be stitched by the veterinary surgeon. Manfred gently held the animal's head, speaking to it soothingly. The vet found that he could work on the leg without the slightest fuss from the horse. Regrettably when Manfred left Rhodesia the horse became unmanageable once more and had to be put down.

Circumstances now began to change Manfred's life dramatically. In 1933 he went down with a bad bout of malaria. The doctor who tended him sent him to Cape Town where he temporarily recovered, but on his return to Umtali it started up again and the doctor had to advise a return to England. Sad at leaving the beautiful African province with its warm climate, the animals and his new found vocation and friends, he left feeling rather low. That summer his mother took him on a tour of Europe. With their mutual love of music they travelled to Bayreuth and Salzburg and then, as she thought it right for him to visit his native land of Bohemia (Czechoslovakia) they went to Prague, staying with friends in that city. Leaving Prague they motored to their beloved Ravello.

Manfred's step-father's influence now took a hand in what was to be a major turning point in his young life. The stories Oliver had told him of his old pilot days had often stirred his imagination and everywhere one turned one found advertisements for young men to join the Royal Air Force. He made up his mind quickly. This could be a great adventure, he thought, and already his head was in the clouds. He applied for a short service commission. Following the usual medicals, interviews and an agonising wait, the official letter was at last in his hand – he had been accepted. He was to commence his training to become a pilot, in the autumn.

That summer the family went to Monte Carlo for a holiday and Manfred and Oliver entered the Alpine Rally. Competing in a two-seater Lancia-Augusta they did in fact win a trophy but before they set off at the start of the rally, Manfred became ill, and a doctor advised him to go to hospital immediately. Manfred refused to do so, not wishing to miss the rally, and, telling no one of his problem, he and Oliver set off from Scotland. Manfred, it was later learned, was in agony the whole way but not for one moment did he let it show. A day or so after the race Oliver had to go to Munich on business, but before he left Manfred finally admitted to him that he was unwell, and he put Manfred straight into hospital. Oliver later joined his wife in Zurich from where they went down to Ravello. Manfred joined them there a few days later and although a doctor friend earnestly advised more hospitalisation, Manfred refused to go and kept on his feet for another two or three days; then he collapsed.

They sent for a nurse from Rome and on the first night, left him in her care. At about 5 am, his mother, feeling uneasy and unable to sleep, went down to his room to see how he was. All was quiet and the nurse who was sitting by his bed, said that he had not moved once. His mother returned to her room but she had a strong feeling that something was wrong, so returned to his room. As she leaned over him she knocked the edge of the bed and Manfred let out a terrific cry of pain, a cry that he had been holding back all night. His mother rushed up stairs to fetch Oliver, who came down while she dressed, then ran down to the Piazza, some fifteen minutes away, to fetch the doctor. The doctor told her to stay and ring through to a specialist in Naples directly the telegraph office opened, while he hurried to the house. Arriving at Manfred's bedside he quickly arranged for a bath of hot water to be prepared and then with Oliver's help, they carried Manfred to it. This was not an easy task, for Manfred was a big man and the bathroom was some distance from his room. All the while Manfred was in terrible pain, yelling like mad, but the hot water seemed to relieve the worst and soon the specialist arrived.

Manfred was very ill all that autumn and his mother remained in Italy to look after him. By Christmas he was well on the road to recovery. Now feeling much better, he went off for a winter holiday to Austria, staying at the beautiful village of St Anton in the Tyrol. He took up skiing again, a sport in which he had not indulged since his youth. This had been in 1921 when his mother had taken him to the Engadine to meet his father, Otto. She had stayed at St Moritz on that occasion while he went to Arosa with his father. Now in Austria again, Manfred had been practising on his skis for three whole days when some friends said they were off on a skiing expedition. He insisted on going with them, although his brother Edmund argued that it was nonsense, but Manfred insisted and as far as he was concerned that was final. Needless to say he came down the mountain on his back!

Manfred's period of illness, had of course, lost for him this opening into the RAF, but fortunately in early 1935 he applied again and was accepted.

CHAPTER THREE

Royal Air Force Pilot

For Manfred the great adventure of flight was about to begin. After successfully completing his basic training and ground instruction (square bashing) at RAF Uxbridge during April and May, he was sent on May 7 to Number 6 Flying Training School (FTS) at Netheravon, Wiltshire, where he remained until the following February. Manfred was known to most people in the RAF at that time as Beckett, although in the front page of his new flying log-book, he wrote boldly his real name and title.

Netheravon was an old World War One aerodrome, with a large undulating flying field overlooking the Salisbury plains. Manfred was with a number of eager young men all thrown together to form Number 1 Training Course, all being very keen to commence their flying instruction. The course members were split up into sections of four, then each group assigned an instructor. Manfred plus three others were put under the charge of Flying Officer David J. Alvey, who himself had only recently arrived from the Central Flying School, following a tour of flying duty in the Middle East. One of the other three in the group was a 19 year old, dark-haired youth named Richard Ayling.

Things soon began to happen. On May 14, only two days after his arrival in Netheravon, Manfred and the others were told to report to the flying field. In the air above the aerodrome, aeroplanes were already up and Manfred's excitement mounted. Standing silently on the grass was the machine in which he was to start his journey to the skies, an Avro 621 'Tutor'. Outside the pilots' hut Flying Officer Alvey stood looking up at the blue sky as Manfred arrived.

'Morning, Beckett. Feeling all right?'

'Yes Sir,' replied Manfred, pulling nervously at his gloves.

'Right then. We'll just do a circuit or two and show you the local area, OK?' Manfred nodded and said yes. There seemed little else to say.

Alvey indicated the parachute on a chair outside the hut and Manfred sat quickly down onto the pack, fixing the shoulder straps and leg straps to the centre release lock mechanism, pulling them tight.

'Pull those straps really tight, Beckett. We don't want any accidents if you have to jump.'

Standard humour, thought Manfred, knowing only too well what part of his anatomy would bear the brunt of any sudden jerk when a parachute canopy arrested a downward plunge of the body. He pulled the straps tight, so tight that he could not stand in an upright position when he finally heaved himself from the chair. He recalled at ground school a humorous, red-faced flight sergeant saying something about being a candidate for the WAAFs if one jumped out of an aeroplane with the parachute's leg straps, which went under the crutch, too loose. Everyone had laughed, but at least it was more original than the joke about bringing the parachute back should it fail to open properly if one should bale out! Still it was an improvement on the old type of harness where the two leg straps snapped onto hooks at the front. You could, however, walk along without being bent double. With progress though, one lost the old nostalgic sound of those two hooks making one of those pleasant clinking sounds that brought back memories for the older generation of flyers.

Alvey walked over to the Avro, waving briefly to the mechanic that he was going up. Manfred waddled after him wondering why he had to go through this embarrassing scene, not being able to stand upright, while the parachute pack banged the back of his knees. Alvey's parachute was in the rear cockpit, where an airman helped him to strap it to his backside as he strapped himself to the aeroplane. Manfred climbed up awkwardly into the front cockpit, noticing how nobody helped him. All part of the game, he supposed.

In a second, however, all this was forgotten. He was seated in the Tutor and was about to fly. For the first time that smell of an aeroplane came to him. A sweet mixture of castor oil, with a faint metallic tang, delicately mixed with fabric dope, and petrol, invaded his senses. Looking about the cockpit he noticed the chipped paint on the metal parts and the odd trace of mud on the cockpit floor. In front of him was an array of instruments. He tried to remember them. Yesterday he knew them all but today the names and their function seemed to escape him. The one immediately ahead of him was the artificial horizon, he always remembered that one because of the little aeroplane on it, but the others ....

The engine bursting into life brought his mind back to what was happening about him. An airman jumped up on the wing, checking Manfred's straps. So they did think about him after all!

'All OK, Sir?' Manfred gave a professional thumbs-up sign and the airman vanished. Alvey's voice came over the Gosport tube, a device invented at Gosport which enabled the pilot and pupil to speak to each other.

'Just watch the instruments, Beckett, see what I do and don't touch the controls unless I tell you to, OK?' Manfred nodded.

'OK!?'

'OK, Sir,' yelled Manfred feeling foolish, expecting Alvey to hear his nod! Manfred adjusted the tube and prepared himself for take-off. The Gosport tube was a simple yet useful piece of invention. Wound from metal strips, making flexible pipes that were bound with black cotton, they ran from one cockpit to the other. The instructor spoke into a rubber mouthpiece at one end while the pupil could listen through earpieces at the other end. A second tube allowed the pupil to reverse this procedure. Simple, and with no working parts and no electrical contrivances to go wrong, it was quite effective.

Alvey waved away the mechanics and pulled his goggles over his eyes, Manfred too quickly covered his own eyes. The Tutor was moving now, bumping slowly across the grass towards the runway. Manfred looked at the instruments trying to remember why the altimeter was not on zero. The bumping stopped; they were on the edge of the runway. Alvey was looking round, waiting for another Tutor that was coming down to land. They both watched as the other aeroplane made a perfect landing ten feet above the ground and then slammed down onto the runway. Another young pilot doing his second solo flight! The engine roared again, the Tutor began to shake. Another quick look round, above and behind, then they were onto the runway and off. Manfred watched the ground rushing by, the grass becoming a green blur. Far to his left he could see other pupils in front of the pilots' hut watching. Not watching him particularly, just watching another Tutor take to the sky.

Suddenly they left the ground, the grass and the runway dropping away behind them. The blunt-nosed, silver biplane curved sweetly into the air while Manfred watched the hazy horizon tilt at an unusual angle as Alvey began a smooth, gradual climbing turn, following the aerodrome circuit. They were now at 600 feet, below them stretched the rolling greens and browns of the Wiltshire plains. The 240 hp Armstrong Siddeley 'Lynx' engine purred sweetly as Alvey throttled back after the initial climb. Manfred watched the needle of the airspeed indicator hover on the 100 mph mark, listening to the wind whistling through the wires and struts between the fabric covered, silver-doped wings. Alvey's voice again shocked Manfred back into reality.

'Take the control column and hold the aeroplane steady,' said Alvey in his Irish brogue, 'Gently, gently! Just with the fingertips, don't grab at it like a beer mug handle. That's it, just keep her steady and don't let the nose drop too much.'

Alvey took back the stick a few moments later, flying two more circuits before he began to let down towards the runway. Only minutes later they were down and the engine fell silent. Later Manfred made his first entry in his pilot's flying log-book:

May 14th. Tutor K3391 Pilot: F/O Alvey. Passenger: Self. 30 mins.

Netheravon & District.

Things now began to happen fast in Manfred's training, the entries in his flying log began to grow, together with the number of minutes and hours on dual instruction. David Alvey was pleased with his progress although Manfred was only an average pupil. The good weather continued and soon the trainee pilot was handling the Tutor with growing skill. Exactly two weeks after his first instructional flight, May 28, Alvey took off on what appeared to be just another routine training flight. Another circuit, thought Manfred, as he took the Tutor steadily round the aerodrome, then came gently down into the final approach. The wheels of the fixed undercarriage caressed the runway and the engine was throttled back. Alvey took control, taxied to the dispersal area and stopped. Without cutting the engine he climbed out of his cockpit taking his parachute with him. Heaving the 'chute over his left shoulder in a nonchalant manner he carelessly looked around the sky.

'All right, Beckett, take her round once and keep your eyes open for other aeroplanes.'

Manfred knew that this moment had been fast approaching but Alvey's words stung him into action. The aeroplane's mechanics unrolled the tapes from the interplane struts so that they acted as streamers in the slipstream. This was the signal to others in the air that this pupil was going solo, a sort of airborne 'L' plate – keep clear!

Manfred opened the throttle, looking about to ensure there were no other machines in his path. The Avro rolled towards the end of the runway and as he turned the machine he saw Alvey standing in front of the hut, taking off his flying overalls. Two or three other pilots had seen the usual charade that preceded a pupil's first solo flight and were also watching. Watching Manfred, not just watching another aeroplane take-off. Having completed his final checks and searched the sky for approaching aircraft, he turned onto the runway. It stretched away before him. This was the moment. Could he do it? Alvey thought so. The face of his step-father flashed before him in his mind's eye as he opened the throttle wide. The Tutor moved forward gathering speed; it began to wobble, Manfred rapidly began to think to himself –

'Adjust the feet on the rudder pedals, watch the airspeed, hold the stick steady ... 40 mph ... 50 mph ... keep her steady ... steady.'

The wheels left the ground, touched again briefly then the Tutor was flying.

'Back with the stick ... steady ... gently, up she comes ... gently. Stick now forward a little to gain flying speed. Airspeed OK, horizon steady ... now begin to climb. Revs. OK ... 600 feet ... turn gently to the right ... good, keep her climbing ... all right so far.'

All Manfred's past instruction raced through his brain as he tried to concentrate on flying the Avro. He stole a quick look from the instrument panel, yes he was where he was supposed to be.

'900 feet,' Manfred thought, 'turn to the right again, ... level out ... throttle back, needle resting on 70 mph ... that'll do ... keep her there.'

The aeroplane slipped away to his right as he glanced down. It seemed ages since he took off. Time now to turn again and lose height. He turned steadily, pushing the stick forward ... 500 feet ... 400 feet. Making a final turn into the approach, he saw the runway come into view. This was the tricky bit, he thought. He'd done it

Pilot Officer Manfred Czernin, Royal Air Force, 1936.

Manfred aged six years with Leo. Animals were always a part of his life.

At Oundle School, his arm having been injured in a lathe, summer 1927.

Manfred while working on Colonel Valentine's plantation in Rhodesia, 1932, aged 19.

With Lazaro at Ravello. Most of his holidays were spent in Italy, at beautiful Ravello.

before but suddenly he fully realized that Alvey was not with him His mouth was dry ... 300 feet ... 200 feet ..., he was too high, go round again. No, reduce speed. Good, that's better, everything's all right, here comes the runway ... give her power, ease back with the stick ....

The end of the runway slipped under the leading edges of his lower wings then the wheels touched. Alvey watched as his pupil touched down without trouble, came to a halt, then began to taxi off the runway.

'Well, Beckett,' thought Alvey, 'that's the start, now you'll really start to work!'

Manfred soloed again, twice, on the 5th, but this time each flight lasted 15 minutes, not five, as on his first solo in K3434. He was now at home in the Tutor, he liked it.

The Avro Tutor had superseded the Avro 504N as the RAF's principal training aeroplane in 1933, to become standard equipment until 1939. It was, naturally, easy to fly, with a maximum speed of 122 mph, and could cruise happily at 105 mph at 1,000 feet. It could fly for 2¾ hours at a service ceiling of 16,200 feet.

July 26 was a big day, the first solo cross-country flight. Manfred took off from Netheravon in K3391, flying to Abingdon which took 40 minutes, returning without incident in 30 minutes, flying at 2,000 feet the whole way. July 31, and his second cross-country, this time to Gosport and back in 65 minutes, flying in K3392.

Weeks passed and Manfred became more and more proficient in the air, and that summer was one of the happiest of his life. He had captured, as all airmen capture, the love and freedom of the skies. A whole new and exciting world was his, the clouds were his islands to explore. He was a pilot!

Flying practice followed lecture, lecture followed flying. Hours began to mount both in the air and in the classroom. The classroom part was perhaps the most trying for the pupils who paid little real attention to the more academic side of flight study. They would much rather be out 'poleing' a Tutor around the sky.

Aerobatics were eventually conquered and gradually the student pilot began to feel a certain mastery over his aeroplane. The loop became a pleasant manoeuvre. Control column slightly forward to gain speed, a quick glance around the sky to see that all was clear, throttle open then pull back the stick, keep the rudder bar control and over she goes. The horizon drops away, blue sky, a flash of sunlight, more blue sky, head back, watch for the horizon to appear but up-side-down, then as the earth comes back to where it should be, level out. Rolling to the left had its problems. When doing a roll to the right it was easy with the right hand holding the stick, the left hand on the throttle control. When trying a roll to the left, however, one never seemed to be able to reach far enough to push the stick into the left hand, forward position in the cockpit, so one had to change hands for an instant and forget the throttle. In the trainee's early attempts it usually ended up with the machine plunging round and then hurtling out of the roll in any odd direction with the airspeed approaching 120 mph. Practice, however soon overcame these predicaments.

The one fellow trainee that Manfred teamed up with was an Irishman named Cooper. They would often be seen together although their backgrounds and temperaments were very different. Another friend was Richard Ayling. Ayling had lived in south London, so whenever they went home at weekends, Manfred would drive to his mother's house in York Terrace, taking Richard with him. Manfred drove a splendid Wolseley Hornet which was much admired by his companions. Manfred would leave Richard in south London with instructions for him to meet him at 11 pm Sunday night for the drive back to Netheravon. More often than not, Richard would have to wait and wait until Manfred finally arrived, probably well after midnight, from some party or nightclub. Manfred by this time would be well inebriated, would motion his friend into the driving seat, then flop down in the passenger seat to fall fast asleep, leaving Richard to drive them both back to Wiltshire.

To his colleagues of No 1 Course, Manfred soon became the object of much curiosity plus a certain amount of admiration. He certainly moved in very different circles than most of them, also having his share of female companions.

One of these ladies was the wife of a flight commander. Manfred let this slip to Richard Ayling who frankly found it difficult to believe. However, a few days later he borrowed Manfred's car, which he often did. Manfred kept the Hornet in the local village and that evening Ayling went down into Netheravon to collect it. In the semi-gloom of evening Richard seated himself behind the steering wheel and was just about to start the engine when the lady in question came up to the car. In the poor light she mistook Richard for Manfred and her opening remark left no doubt in Richard's mind that Manfred's story had been true. It was most embarrassing but shortly afterwards the story had an amusing sidelight when the flight commander found his wife and Manfred together. The amusing thing was that the man, apparently without too much fuss or bother, offered and then drove Manfred back to the station.

Another girl-friend was taken for a drive one day but Manfred had to report to Netheravon, and so left her on top of a hill in the middle of nowhere, promising to be back to pick her up in an hour, after showing his face in the mess. Imagine her state when after leaving her at about 11 am, he didn't return until about 7 pm that evening. Apparently the friendship did not progress much further.

Manfred was not the only one to be in trouble. One evening Richard Ayling again borrowed Manfred's car, and to his great embarrassment, managed to put it into a ditch. Returning from an evening out with another pal and both their respective girl-friends, the front wheels, always on the light side, became even more so with the extra weight in the back, and the Hornet just didn't make a sudden sharp bend in the road.

By the end of the summer, Manfred could do almost everything with the Tutor, then in October he came near to flying service aeroplane types. In that month he began to convert to the Hawker Hart Trainer, a fast racy aeroplane compared with the Tutor. Certain things had to be learnt all over again. Spinning – nice and slow with full opposite rudder to make the Hart come out of it. Landing could be a bit dicey on windy days for one had to pull back the stick that last little bit in quick time or the Hart would drop onto her springy undercarriage, to bounce five or six feet back into the air. A quick burst of power and she would sink down again without further trouble.

The service Hart had been the standard two-seat light day bomber in the RAF since 1931, both this and the training version being powered by 525 hp Rolls Royce Kestrel X engines.

Over the latter months of 1935, Manfred safely transferred to the Hart, flying more adventurous cross-country flights, bombing theory and aerobatics.

For the young pilots of the mid-1930's, service in the Royal Air Force was a very happy life, living in the officers' Mess being a main feature. It was all very civilised, with batmen, waiters and all the mod cons of a first-class hotel, but with a more happy and relaxed atmosphere, and they were being paid too! Breakfast started the day off well, with the older hands and instructors busily engaged over bacon and eggs, or sausages and soggy scrambled-eggs with watery tomatoes, reading newspapers propped up against tea or coffee pots in front of them. (Newspapers could only be read at table at breakfast). Lunch and dinner had full and varied menus and of course, coffee in the ante-room, where talking shop was forbidden, but one could flop down and relax in the dark green leather arm-chairs or settees. The life was one which suited Manfred very well indeed.

On February 5, 1936, the Chief Flying Instructor, Squadron Leader Lydford, went aloft with Manfred as a preliminary to his final assessment at the end of the training course. Squadron Leader Lydford was satisfied, so Manfred passed. At the end of the course, Manfred was assessed as 'Average', with '... no special faults, but he needs close supervision.'

There followed a period of waiting until postings to operational units were announced but it was not long. Within a few days his name appeared on the school's notice board.

Pilot Officer Beckett posted to 57 Squadron RAF.

His friend Richard Ayling received his posting too, being sent to No 3 (Fighter) Squadron, to fly the Hawker Fury.

57 Squadron was a day bomber unit equipped with the Hawker Hart two-seat bomber and on joining them he was assigned to B Flight. The squadron was stationed at Upper Heyford, Oxfordshire, where it had been based since 1932.

The service Hart was no different from the training version, except that it was armed with a forward firing Vickers Gun and a rear Lewis Gun in the rear cockpit. It could carry a bomb load of 500 pounds but it was only practice bombs that were carried.

Manfred settled in happily enough and began to enjoy squadron life as a pilot. Soon rumours began to circulate that their Harts were shortly to be replaced by the faster Hawker Hind. It was one rumour that proved correct, the crews converting onto the new aeroplane type which began to arrive during May.

After a few weeks on the squadron, Manfred was finally allowed to put up his pilot's Wings. Unlike the later system of a formal parade with some VIP ceremoniously pinning the coveted flying brevet to a proud and heaving left breast, in the 1930's orders just came through official channels. The young pilot would race to his room, take off his old tunic and put on the one to which he had already had his Wings stitched. For the next couple of weeks or so the young eagle would strut about slightly taller and with his left breast slightly forward and always placed at a strategic angle so all could see his most prized possession. All this display was not unnatural and the bravado soon wore off.

Following the conversion onto Hinds, Manfred was posted, going to the RAF depot at Uxbridge in June, for further ground instruction. One wonders if one of Manfred's slight indiscretions had caught up with him or perhaps his masters' displeasure had been aroused.

However, he took advantage of this break to take a course in Italian. This later led, in January 1937, to his becoming a Second Class Interpreter in this, his childhood-learnt language. Little did he know then, to what use this knowledge of the Italian language would be put in the not-too-distant future.

Manfred remained at Uxbridge until December when he received a posting to 83 Squadron in 2 Group, Bomber Command, and stationed at Turnhouse, Midlothian just outside Edinburgh. 83 Squadron had been reformed that August and although officially a Hind unit it possessed a couple of Harts on its strength. Manfred was welcomed by the Commanding Officer, Squadron-Leader Dermot A. Boyle, being immediately accepted into his new squadron.

The Hawker Hind was going through an initial period of trivial technical troubles at this time, but this soon passed, allowing more and more aeroplanes to become fully operational. Training for Manfred, as for every pilot, continued even on a service squadron, with formation flying, camera-gun practice, low level bombing, formation take-offs, landing and dive-bombing. Manfred liked the Hind. After the Hawker Hart it was fast and in many ways a more refined aircraft. Manfred flew as much as weather permitted during the early months of 1937. In March, 83 Squadron went to Leuchars, Fife, for a practice camp which lasted for just over three weeks. His usual rear-gunner was Corporal Parker. He flew some 27 hours during the camp and his total flying hours mounted to just under 190.

Dermot Boyle, later Marshal of the Royal Air Force Sir Dermot

Boyle, remembers Manfred vividly as a very likeable and personable young man. Like many young pilots, Manfred was always living life to the full, racing off to London whenever he could get away at weekends, driving madly back to Scotland after a very full and hectic two days, then taking pep-pills to keep himself awake when back on duty.

The authority and advice given to Manfred by his Squadron Commander was not always well received, but then youth rarely takes heed of wisdom of their elders. Even so, for Boyle, trying to mould each individual character into a first-rate airman, yet hoping not to curb too much the flamboyant nature which each man created within himself, was not an easy task. It was also his job to keep each man alive, not altogether a simple task when giving a young man not far removed from the restrictions of parental and scholastic control a powerful aircraft. This is the time, when he has still very much to learn, that he is most vulnerable to error and often, that one error can prove fatal.

A brother pilot in 83 Squadron was Denis Lyster, who was perhaps a little nearer to Manfred than Squadron Leader Boyle could be, although Manfred rarely became really close in friendship, being far too independent for that. Lyster, at that time a sergeant pilot, but later a Group Captain with the DSO, DFC and AFC, recalls:

'The general impression we squadron pilots had of him was that no one could make much impression on him, and regardless of whatever briefing, no one was sure of what interpretation Czernin would place upon information or advice. Consequently there was a bit of trepidation, to say the least, amongst the ground crew and pilots alike, whenever he took to the air. His analysis of a situation and method of execution was unpredictable – to the extent that any exercise of which he was leader, caused considerable laughter and ribaldry amongst those not directly involved. It is only fair to say that many of us were inexperienced in those pre-war years and independence of thought and action often gave the best results. Manfred was quite fearless and caution seemed to be unknown to him.'

While he was no doubt liked and probably secretly admired by some members of the squadron, he was too unpredictable to become really close to anyone. Even so, he did possess a warmth of character and understanding, and it was obvious to Denis Lyster at least, that he had many of the real qualities needed in the RAF. To sum up Lyster's general impression:

'He liked fast cars and fast aeroplanes – his personality was outside the realm of convention.'

During May Manfred was sent on long cross-country flights from Turnhouse to West Freugh and back. On other flights he would travel up to Usworth or Aberdeen. On June 2 he flew a Hind (K6635) with a full war load plus Corporal Beattie seated in the rear cockpit. The object of the exercise was a height test, the two men reaching 20,000 ft, which was the highest Manfred had ever flown. On the 15th he went south on attachment to RAF Biggin Hill in Kent, staying until the 25th.

With the summer weather, flying increased. In July 83 Squadron were requested to provide aeroplanes for a Royal Escort on the occasion of King George VI's visit to Belfast and Northern Ireland. 83 flew on attachment to Aldergrove on the 25th, flying rehearsal flights on the 26th and 27th. The fly-past took place on the 28th, Manfred being chosen to fly in the formation. Flying in K6636 with Aircraftsman Rennie behind, and led by 83's new CO Squadron Leader Leonard Snaith, the formation flew over the Royal Yacht as the King and Queen made their way up Belfast Lough. Manfred kept station to the left of his Flight Commander, Flight Lieutenant A. W. Vincent. He looked down at the yacht as the Hinds swept over, a feeling of immense pride welling up inside him. It was a crowning end to Manfred's period of service with the RAF, for he was placed on the Reserve Class A in August 1937.

During his 2½ years with the Service he had amassed a total of 250 hours flying time but was still only assessed as 'Average' when he left. He was naturally a little sad at leaving the Royal Air Force and it was even a sadder time when he learnt that his mother and Oliver had separated. (They were divorced in 1941). He and his mother, therefore, returned to their beautiful Ravello once more.

CHAPTER FOUR

The Last Years of Peace

Manfred was at something of a loose end when he left the Royal Air Force and for a while, following a long holiday at Ravello and returning to London, did nothing very much. He was quite happy to become once again the 'man about town', not that the time spent in the Service stopped him from being the playboy, especially while on leave. He dressed well and was to be seen at all the right places where the Mayfair set were to be seen, and at all the better class gambling clubs. Because of his love of cricket he became a member of the MCC, and it was at Lords that he could be found on sunny Saturday afternoons.

Being at a loose end Manfred got the idea of going to the United States. After the voyage to New York, he travelled overland to California where he stayed with friends of the family. There had been some hope on the part of these friends that a romantic association might develop between Manfred and their daughter but nothing deep came of their friendship. Everyone nevertheless remained the very best of friends.

Following his return to England, Manfred, as a reservist in the RAF, attending his annual reserve training, going to No 5 ERFTS at Hanworth, where he again became the aviator. The Camp began on June 20 and he found that his instructor was none other than Flight Lieutenant D. Davies who had been one of his instructors at Netheravon. Davies checked him out on the Blackburn B2 machine, Manfred going solo on the type the following day. After eleven flights on the Blackburn, Davies took him up in a Hart and a day or so later he flew an Audax. For ten days Manfred once again enjoyed the freedom of the skies going through the very basic flying routine, just to 'keep his hand in', adding twenty flying hours to his overall total. A cross-country flight to Filton and back and a height test on the 30th ended his training and he returned to civilian life once again.

Manfred now decided to go into the restaurant business, asking a close friend to join him in this venture. The friend was Alwyn Bolton, who had lived almost next door to the Frosts in York Terrace. With money supplied, not by the young men themselves naturally, but by their respective mothers, Manfred and Alwyn formed a company named Manfred Limited, leasing premises at 102 Wardour Street, in London's Soho district, and fitted out and finally opened a restaurant-cum-snack-bar which they named The Hot Dog. Manfred had, apparently, been quite impressed with American hamburgers and hot-dogs during his trip to the United States. Thus armed with this enthusiastic idea he had persuaded his friend Alwyn to come in with him in this project.

The two young men, who were neighbours as already mentioned, had been friends for some years. They had met one day when Alwyn, sitting in his mother's house, heard a tremendous crash outside in York Terrace. Rushing out he found a young woman had crashed her sports car into a lamp standard, the standard having fallen over the car but fortunately she had not been seriously hurt. Manfred, also having heard the crash, quickly appeared together with Enrico and rapidly sizing up the situation turned to the young Bolton and said, 'Is she drunk?' After the police etc: had arrived the two men formally introduced themselves, Manfred suggesting that Alwyn should come over and have a drink sometime. Thus a great friendship began.

Alwyn Bolton was just over a year older than Manfred and following his education at Trinity College, Cambridge, had studied to become a barrister, but spent most of his time in the art and antique business. When Manfred later suggested, in 1938, that they start this restaurant idea, Alwyn was only too pleased, thinking that this was by far a more pleasant way of making money.

The Hot Dog was finally ready for business by early December 1938, by which time the two co-directors, Manfred and Alwyn, had persuaded a third man to join them who had the catering background and know-how. This was Ivan Joseph, introduced through a friend of Alwyn's mother. Ivan had previously been with J. Lyons & Co., for seven years. Together with a chef they hired, they formally opened the business on Friday, December 16, 1938.

The grand opening was officiated at by the film actress Miss Helen Terry, who chose jugged hare as her first meal. All the society columns gave good coverage to the new venture and for a while it was quite the thing to visit this Wardour Street snack-bar.

The intention had been to aim at the daily office worker trade, the highest priced meal during the day being 1/9d, while a three course meal cost a mere 1/6d. In addition, the speciality of American hot dogs would hopefully bring in much passing trade to fill the 57 seats available. It was also hoped to have a famous film star or stage personality present themselves each week but this did not work out too well although again the newspaper columns covered the day the actress Gwen Ffrangcon-Davies, the recent star of *Gas-Light* at the Richmond Theatre, visited them. Although no more than a snack-bar, Manfred cheerfully and probably hopefully described the business as trying to 'Combine the dignity of the Ritz with the charm of a Mayfair restaurant.'

Manfred and Alwyn were not, however, anything like real businessmen, really only playing the part. With their constant comings and goings and bringing in a good many non-paying friends as their guests for an evening out, their colleague Ivan Joseph soon became disenchanted with his two partners. As trade slowly began to dwindle they hopefully turned the restaurant's basement area into a bar where businessmen could gather for a chat over a drink. They called this The Alibi, thinking the title both amusing and appropriate but even this did not pull the business into shape and at last, Joseph had had enough of carrying his two playboy colleagues, and left. Shortly after this the business closed and in any event both men were soon in uniform, Manfred in the RAF, and Alwyn, already a member of the Territorial Army, soon off to war with the Royal Artillery.

Manfred and Alwyn remained good friends throughout and after the war. Alwyn was always impressed by his companion's various antics and on his first visit to the Frosts' home his artistic interest was more than aroused when he noticed a Picasso abstract hanging on the wall.

Shortly before The Hot Dog opened, Manfred had, in November 1938, met the woman who was to become his wife. Maud Hamilton was shopping in Good's China Shop in South Audley Street, W1, with her friend and chaperone when Manfred, whom the friend knew, came in. Introductions were made and love blossomed between the playboy Count and the debutante. It was literally love at first sight, which when beautiful can fill the heart. The next evening he invited her to a dance at the Royal Albert Hall. She accepted and that evening their love was sealed.

Maud's mother, however, was not impressed with her only daughter's choice of a boyfriend. Manfred's mother had known Maud's father, Ronald Hamilton, who was a diplomat, years earlier when she had been introduced to him at an embassy cocktail party, while she was still married to Otto Czernin. When Manfred began to see Maud with increasing regularity, Mrs Hamilton became strongly opposed to the idea, especially as her daughter's intended had no real job, little visible means of support, and whose only prospect in sight was that he was about to be a partner in some sort of café. That summer the Hamiltons took Maud with them to Switzerland hoping that the separation would terminate the romance. Manfred was most unhappy with this so his mother packed him off to Ravello for a holiday.

Manfred once again found himself at his favourite second home, the beautiful Italian Villa Cimbrone. Cimbrone had been purchased by his mother's father, Baron Grimthorpe in 1905. The grounds were half of the top of a peninsula sticking out into the sea. The other half was owned by another person, who thinking it might be important and desirable for the Baron to own the whole peninsula offered his half to him for an exorbitant price. Baron Grimthorpe died in May 1917 when his son Ralph was fighting in the Great War, but after the war, Ralph, now the third Baron, and his sister Lucile purchased the second half, divided it between them, and Lucile had built there a beautiful house high on the rock, 1,200 feet above the sea. She named the house Rondinaia, which means Swallow's Nest.

The town of Ravello, overlooking the Gulf of Salerno, is situated between Salerno and Sorrento with the Isle of Capri just along the coast to the west. Naples, to the north, was only a short distance away by car. From that famous and historic town it was a pleasant drive south to Castellammare by the coast road then across country to Amalfi. Looking back one could see mighty Vesuvius on the horizon, before continuing down to Ravello.

In 1955, Mrs Frost was forced to sell the house and land because of rising taxes, cost of upkeep etc; for she could not afford to run houses in both England and Italy. Her brother was also obliged to sell Cimbrone shortly before his death in February 1963.

In August 1939 Manfred was again required for his reserve training and so once again donning his blue Royal Air Force uniform he went off to Hanworth and to No 5 ERFTS, this time to take an Instructor's Course. The world political situation, especially in Europe was daily becoming more critical but in England things seemed little different from previous summers. Children played by the sea, girls and boys walked hand in hand, and cricket was played on village greens. Manfred himself had been convinced for many years that another war with Germany was inevitable. Believing this, he was happy in the knowledge that when and if war came, he was already trained to take part in it.

Manfred arrived at Hanworth on the 14th, and commenced his course, being again checked out on the Blackburn B2s, going solo the next day, then proceeding through the usual practice sorties, then going onto Hawker Harts. All the while and as the course continued it seemed obvious that something was going to happen. Then came Friday September 1. Hitler's armies marched into Poland and two days later Britain was at war with Germany for the second time in twenty-odd years. Manfred, in uniform, was prepared and ready and was in the war from the very first day as he would have wished. He was still to be on active duty six years later when Germany was finally defeated, but he could never have guessed along which paths his war would take him, nor would he ever have guessed where he would be when Germany surrendered.

On Monday September 2, 1939, Manfred, his course terminated due to mobilization, went to No 4 AOS at West Freugh where he was checked out on a Miles Magister and a Hawker Henley. With the Henley and its Rolls Royce Merlin engine he came in close contact for the first time with something very like a modern fighter aeroplane, and he liked it. He had seen the Hurricanes and Spitfires from afar but now he had come close to flying a machine like them. He liked it very much.

The Hamiltons had of course returned to England by this time, and Manfred again met Maud while on leave, before being posted to Pembrey. In that moment when they saw each other again they knew nothing had changed between them. They decided to marry at once at any cost, and it seemed a very real case of now or never. With the war about to explode all over the world it was, for many people, a case of living for the moment, there seeming to be little future for any young men.

After a brief stay at RAF Pembrey, Manfred went to Hucknall on September 22, posted in as a Ferry Pilot. A date was set for the wedding and so Maud ran away from the family house in Westbourne Terrace, Bayswater, to Mrs Frost's London flat, 38 Shrewsbury House, in Cheyne Walk. Two days later Manfred obtained a weekend pass, came to London and the couple were married at the Old Church, Chelsea on November 4. Their old friends the Boltons had moved from York Terrace to 46 Tite Street, off the Chelsea Embankment, and although Alwyn was away in the army, Mrs Bolton held the wedding reception at her home. Algernon Blackwood, the publisher and an old friend of Mrs Frost, gave away the bride, and Manfred's best man was Lord Bill Waleron, another old friend who was about to join the RAFVR. For a short while Maud and Manfred were happy, very happy, but war changes many things and for many people, life was never the same again.

The newlyweds returned to Hucknall in Nottinghamshire, Maud living in digs near the airfield. Life was very different for the young bride, from being a debutante in Mayfair to a housewife in a couple of rooms equipped only with a primus stove, but they were together, and they were in love.

A personal tragedy that came to Mrs Frost and to Manfred the following year was the death of Enrico, the loyal and devoted chauffeur to Mrs Frost and who had been in her service since 1919, and who had for many years been a sort of father figure to Manfred when a boy. In June 1940 when Italy declared war on the Allies, Enrico, being an Italian citizen was arrested. Along with others deemed 'undesirable aliens' he was shipped to Canada, but the ship in which he sailed was torpedoed and sunk. So died the one man who was so near to Manfred and who had been such a friend to him. In the months that followed, when Manfred was flying in action, he was later to confide to his mother that whenever he was in the air, especially in times of danger, he always felt that Enrico was with him, guiding him, protecting him. He would be with him again during the latter years of the war in Italy, when he was to be in a very different kind of danger.

CHAPTER FIVE

The Battle of France

Hitler's war was the turning point in many people's lives. Things would never be the same for anyone again and for Manfred Czernin, the gay, flamboyant days of the thirties were past. Life took on a serious look but Manfred was grateful that if there was to be a war, at least he was trained and ready for it. Personally he saw the war as a tremendous challenge, a new adventure, a chance to prove himself; he was eager to get into action. In this he was, like many others, to be initially frustrated for the shooting war just did not start. All remained quiet.

On September 22 Manfred was sent to No. 1 Ferry Pilot's Pool at RAF Hucknall, and not to an operational squadron as he had hoped. As soon as he realized that he was not missing anything, he was satisfied to at least be flying. During the first months of the war he flew Ansons, Queen Bees, Tiger Moths and Fairey Battle bombers, ferrying them to various units up and down the country. All the while, he was hoping for an operational posting to come through but feared that when it did come it would be to a bomber squadron, for after all he had been trained as a bomber pilot.

He therefore applied for an interview with Air Vice Marshal Trafford Leigh-Mallory, Officer Command Fighter Command's 12 Group, formally requesting a posting to a fighter unit. Whether Leigh-Mallory saw something in Manfred's keen eyes we shall never know, but his request was, subject to aptitude, granted. In December he went to 12 Group's Fighter Pool at Aston Down for assessment, and here spent the war's first Christmas. He was more than a little worried about his future, for not only did he feel that his bomber training might still go against him, but he was now only a month away from his 27th birthday, and this was old for a fighter pilot.

He flew his first single-engined fighter – a Gloster Gladiator Biplane – and at once he was 'lost'. It felt good. Again came that certain feeling of great freedom as he soared above the clouds in a machine that, like himself, was soon to make a name for itself in this war. Early in January he took his final tests and the Commanding Officer of the Fighter Pool, Wing Commander B. Caswell, made the assessment that was to change Manfred's life. In Manfred's flying log-book the Wing Commander wrote: 'Assessed ability as Fighter Pilot – above the Average. 14. 1. 40.'

By this time Manfred had over 300 flying hours to his credit and England would soon, very soon, need all her fighter pilots.

Manfred received his posting shortly afterwards, to 504 Fighter Squadron based at Debden arriving on January 23, with Pilot Officer Renison and Pilot Officer Wendel. With 504 he was to convert onto the Hawker Hurricane. He was impressed with the machine. When he prepared for his first flight he felt a kind of excited reverence towards it. It was his first monoplane fighter and, with the Supermarine Spitfire, it was the last word in fighters. The Hurricane was big, powerful looking, and it felt and smelt like a warplane. He strapped himself in as his instructor gave him the rundown on the cockpit layout, what to do, what to watch for, but Manfred was way ahead of him – in his own mind he was already flying.

'To close the shutters of the coolant, you ...'

The Hurricane began to move forward, the Merlin engine roaring.

'Remember to watch the boost control ...'

The wheels left the ground and the machine began to climb.

'Top speed is about 330 mph ...'

Manfred curved the Hurricane deep into the grey sky; she was great and he could feel the warmth and strength of the machine like that of a warrior queen. As he broke through clouds into the blue world above he suddenly knew that at last he had reached the goal in life, that until that moment, he had not dreamed of. He was a fighter pilot.

In February he went to 213 Squadron at Wittering becoming an operational pilot. On the 14th he had his first action. Flying from Cromer to Sutton Bridge he saw a twin-engined machine and gave chase, but when he closed he identified it as a British Blenheim.

There followed a period of intense training, formation practice, firing at ground targets and at towed drogues. Practice scrambles, aerobatics and mock interceptions and dog-fights. This was interspersed with convoy patrols with always the slight chance of action, but none came. In France the air war had started, already the Royal Air Force had fought with enemy aircraft and surely something must happen soon.

Early in May, Manfred changed units again, this time going to 85 Squadron who were in France. Manfred moved nearer to the war, soon he would be able to prove himself in combat. He arrived at his new unit on May 9, 1940, and the following day the Germans launched their offensive. The so called Phoney War was over and the shooting war began.

85 Squadron was commanded by Squadron Leader John O. W. Oliver and was one of the two Hurricane squadrons with the Air Component, the other being 87 Squadron. These two units had seen little real action since arriving in France in September 1939, but the two Hurricane squadrons with the Advanced Air Striking Force, 1 and 73, had, however, already more than proved themselves against the Luftwaffe.

Twenty one years before, in 1918, 85 Squadron had first gone into action on the Western Front flying SE5A biplane scouts, armed with one Vickers and one Lewis machine guns. Now it was equipped with the Hurricane Mark 1, carrying eight Browning machine guns. It was fast, could take a great deal of punishment and look after itself in combat.

The day after Manfred joined 85 the Germans began their massive attacks into Holland, Belgium and Luxembourg in a bid to by-pass and go around the French defences on the Maginot Line. At once the RAF squadrons were in the thick of the fighting and were almost immediately re-inforced by other units from England.

85 Squadron were in action at once on that first day. Squadron Leader Oliver shot down a Heinkel 111 bomber, Flight Lieutenant Boothby got two Junker 88's, John Hemingway, LePine and Pane also destroyed Heinkels, Ashton and Blair each downing two. Flight Sergeant Sammy Allard, who was to become one of the most outstanding of the squadron's pilots, also got a Heinkel and damaged another. Flight Lieutenant Lee and two other pilots claimed a Junkers 86 while yet other pilots claimed one enemy bomber as probably destroyed and damaged others. For the next eight days the pilots were in action every day, gaining victories and

losing pilots. Manfred, however, got off to a bad start, and it was partly his own fault.

For some reason best known to himself, Manfred was a great romancer and story-teller. He usually did it merely for effect, probably to enjoy the reaction of people suddenly confronted with some fantastic tale which they naturally believed. This sort of thing often got him into all sorts of trouble, but he always laughed it off, and all his tales were so easy to disprove, but by that time he had had [illegible]ment of fun.

No sooner had he arrived in France than his brother pilots no doubt became interested in this new man with an odd-sounding name and a count too. It is easy to imagine their enquiring glances until someone finally asked the question. What nationality are you? Where did you learn to fly? You're not English, are you?

Manfred was quick to spot his entrance for a story, or was it in fact his way of putting them in their place. Whatever the real reason, he found that on this occasion it back-fired on him. He told them that he had previously served in the Luftwaffe and had flown the Messerschmitt bf 109, Germany's latest single-seater fighter. After that they tended to steer clear; why, he was almost an enemy! Then it happened. His machine was damaged and he had to force land at another airfield. With communications strained and the forces being in a very busy but confused state he was missing for three days. His CO, John Oliver, remembers being questioned by the Intelligence people who obviously hearing the story of his Luftwaffe service, were wondering if he had indeed gone back to his former masters. Manfred then returned, sorted out the mystery and was back in action the following day.

Manfred's first successful air action came on May 19, having up until this time merely stayed alive in his first encounters, which was not an unimportant consideration.

On the 19th he was flying at 19,000 ft with the squadron when they spotted a large formation of German bombers, mostly Heinkels, escorted by Messerschmitt fighters which weaved and darted about above and behind their charges. Manfred switched his gun from 'safe' to 'fire' and began to search the sky about him, making sure no other fighters were about. Then the Hurricanes were diving down, making for the bombers. Sergeant Howitt was slightly ahead of him and already firing. The bomber's rear gunners were also firing now, and the criss-cross of tracer bullets began to fill the air. Manfred selected a target, closed in quickly, suddenly realizing he was coming in much too fast and quickly throttled back. The Hurricane lost speed and seemed to drop slightly but Manfred jabbed at the gun button and the machine shook with the recoil of its eight guns. The German aircraft turned and dropped its right wing, Manfred following firing again. Smoke was now pouring from one engine and the enemy pilot was obviously in trouble. Slamming open the throttle, Manfred sped after his target and fired again. Now both engines were ablaze and a parachute appeared. No time for elation over his first kill, for already he was curving in behind another bomber which also went down under his fire.

By this date, John Oliver had returned to England, 85 having been taken over by Squadron Leader Mike Peacock DFC, a South African. Peacock had led the attack, and shot down the leading bomber but was then himself shot down and had to bale out.

Mike Peacock, a pre-war Auxiliary pilot who had flown with 601 Squadron, later reported back and told his men that:

'I shot down the leading Heinkel so that all the others who had been too busy formating to look at their maps, would then get lost.'

85 Squadron had again been successful, for during the day its pilots had claimed 16 enemy aircraft for certain with others unconfirmed or damaged. Pilot Officer A. G. Lewis, a young South African, had personally claimed five of these, while Pat Woods-Scowen got four, including three Me109's. Sergeant Howitt had destroyed a Heinkel and Sergeant Little claimed two victories.

For Manfred it was a personal triumph, for he had more than proved himself this day. His first Heinkel had been seen to go down and crash and had thus been confirmed although his second kill went down without being witnessed and as yet was still unconfirmed.

Later in the day he made up for this when, with other members of the squadron, he intercepted a formation of Dornier 17 bombers. Near Lille they dived headlong into the enemy, Manfred once again feeling the recoil of his eight machine-guns, seeing his fire chew into the German aeroplane which exploded and fell. Pulling up he curved down behind another Dornier, whose rear gunner was pumping shells at him as he closed in. Manfred's first burst silenced the gunner but the Dornier was turning. Manfred turned with it, aimed a perfect deflection burst which set the port motor ablaze. The Dornier hung for a moment then began to fall away in a tight turn,

Manfred close behind, emptying his guns into the grey-green fuselage, seeing bits flying off before the burning wing ripped away, flipping the Dornier onto its back, in which attitude it hit the earth below.

Manfred climbed away into a strangely silent sky, giving one quick glance back at the black column of smoke rising from his fourth victory of the day. Four kills in one day, three being officially confirmed, was good work. This is what his training had all been about, this is what his life had been leading to. There was for him only one thing better than being a fighter pilot and that was being a successful fighter pilot. Now he had destroyed his first enemies in air combat and had survived the dangers. He hoped that this success might last a little longer.

The next day, May 20, the air actions continued, patrols also being flown over the advancing enemy columns. Over the front Manfred spotted a single-engined Henschel 126, a light two-seat army observation aeroplane, spotting for the German troops. The two-seater was no match for Manfred's Hurricane, the British pilot blasting it from the sky. The kill came easily but the two men had to die.

All through the day, reports came in concerning the rapid advance of the Germans. At 1330, Squadron Leader Peacock gave the adjutant, Flying Officer T. J. Molony, orders to destroy all the Squadron files, records, cyphers etc, and to jettison all kit belonging to airmen and officers, and to have the men ready to move off to Boulogne in 30 minutes. The remaining Hurricanes were serviced and made ready for an attack on the advancing Germans, a skeleton ground crew remaining behind as the main squadron moved off shortly after 1400 hours.

At 1500 hours, Peacock, Manfred and Pilot Officer R. W. Shrewsbury took off in the first available Hurricanes to attack enemy troops near Arras. Manfred, who knew the locality better than his Commanding Officer, led the sortie and soon they spotted the advancing German soldiers, tanks, half-tracks and other assorted vehicles.

Several times the three Hurricanes swooped down, their guns sending out streams of death. When Manfred's guns fell silent he pulled up and climbed away only to find himself alone. Peacock, he later learned, had fired into a petrol tanker which exploded as he roared over it and his Hurricane had turned over and dived into the ground. Richard Shrewsbury too was hit by ground fire and also died.

Manfred landed back alone. His Hurricane was refuelled and then with three other machines were flown off at 1800 as escort to two transport aircraft which flew out the remaining ground crews. Manfred and the remaining aircrew returned to England via Boulogne, and Dover. The adjutant with the road party arrived at Boulogne at 1830 having had their journey hampered by roads choked by refugees. They had to stay in the town overnight, being subjected to an enemy air-raid, before being able to sail to Dover the next day.

Manfred was considerably shaken up by the experiences of those last few days in France; Alwyn Bolton recalls that he heard that Manfred was all in and feeling that nothing could now stop the Germans, either in France or Britain.

85 Squadron too had been shaken up. During the period May 10 to 20, they had lost nine pilots killed or missing, another had been taken prisoner while five others had been wounded. Another pilot had died and another had been injured in a car accident. On the credit side, at least 89 German aeroplanes had been shot down. Squadron Leader Peter Townsend, DFC, took command of 85 on May 23 but Manfred left the unit on May 27 to return to the fighting in France. Squadron Leader John Oliver, Manfred's CO, and who won both the DSO and DFC leading his squadron, remembers Manfred as a '... polished and personable young man,' and recalls, 'a pleasant conversation with him on the subject of skiing, in the Mess at Merville.'

Peter Townsend, who only knew him for a few days, although he was to hear of some of his exploits later in the Battle of Britain, remembers him only briefly for his '... striking appearance and somewhat lisping speech.'

Manfred had lost his flying log-book in France and so he began a new one. Townsend confirmed Manfred's victory tally on the first page and wrote – 'Good luck to you.' Manfred would soon need all the luck he could get.

Having been in action for a little over two weeks, Manfred was, compared with other pilots in 85, in no way 'war-weary' and so he was immediately assigned back to France to join another squadron. He joined 17 Squadron on June 8, also a Hurricane unit arriving with Pilot Officer D. H. Wissler, also from 85 Squadron. After being in action over the beaches during the Dunkirk evacuation, 17 Squadron had been sent to France to join the Advanced Air Striking Force units who were still operating to the south west of Paris. The duty of the squadron, in company with 242 Squadron, was to provide air cover for the ports of Cherbourg and St Malo while the British troops still in France were evacuated to England.

Manfred flew out to join 17 based at Le Mans on June 9, stopping at RAF Kenley to refuel. That same afternoon he flew on patrol with his new unit, a mission flown between Rouen and Le Havre.

One pilot who remembers Manfred's arrival was Harold Bird-Wilson, a young Pilot Officer who had already seen action over Dunkirk: 'His appearance was a welcome change from the normal run of the mill person. Being slightly older than the majority of us, he had a well-matured outlook on life and was a person who knew his way around and was not afraid to express himself. He had the confidence and self-assurance which we were all looking for. I thought him to be rather debonair and will always remember him using a Dunhill cigarette holder for his incessant smoking habits. This habit could have given one the impression of slight nervousness, but on the other hand, at that time it seemed to be the "Mayfair air" that was impressive.'

It would seem that by this time his smoking had become part of his personality.

Life in France from the 8th to 15th June 1940 was, on the whole, pretty chaotic. Since late May the squadron had gone through a succession of commanding officers and its new CO was Squadron Leader Ralph I. G. MacDougall. The unit moved around like gypsies, sleeping in tents or on the floor of farm buildings. Some of their landing grounds used for re-fuelling were just wheat fields that had quickly and sometimes inadequately been surveyed for the purpose.

During June 10 and 11, Manfred flew five patrols, mostly in the Rouen area where most of the squadron's sorties were flown. One patrol over Le Havre attracted very heavy AA fire but nobody was hit. The next day, June 12, the squadron was sent to Mathieu from where it was ordered to patrol St Valerie. On the way three He111K's were encountered bombing troop ships off Le Havre, at the mouth of the River Seine. All three were shot down. Manfred found another scudding through clouds nearby which he engaged, claiming it as destroyed, to make four victories for the squadron.

More patrols and escorts took place on the 13th and 14th, and during the second patrol on the 14th they ran into five

Messerschmitt 109's. The patrol had taken off from Mathieu, their advanced base, code named 'Victor', at 1530 hours to patrol the Seine Estuary at 3,000 ft. At this height they observed three Me109s flying in a vic formation at 4,000 ft. The Messerschmitts saw the Hurricanes, dived and then climbed up again. Manfred was flying as Blue One, with Bird-Wilson as his number two; each attacked a 109 and both began to leave a trail of greyish smoke. Pilot Officer Hanson went after the third enemy fighter and this too went down with black smoke pouring from it. Pilot Officer Ross (Green Two) climbed to 7,000 ft and found two more 109's, hit one with all his ammunition sending it down in a steep dive but he did not see it crash. Pilot Officer Leary attacked what he reported to be a He112, but without result.

Back at base, Manfred was amazed that only 30 minutes had elapsed since he and the others had taken off. All three pilots who had seen their opponents go down made claims but they were not confirmed, and so Manfred's personal score during the Battle of France remained at five destroyed plus two more unconfirmed.

By now the Army had moved back, leaving a considerable amount of equipment and stores behind them, amongst which were a number of motor-cycles. The squadron personnel 'acquired' these and staged mock races around the nearby Le Mans racing circuit without any serious damage to themselves, before finally destroying them when they had to pull out. They also found in the NAAFI store situated in the stands at Le Mans, vast quantities of cigarettes and spirits which they felt obliged to liberate. This led to the squadron being able to stock up with these valuable items rather than personal equipment, before proceeding to a new base at Dinard.

The move to Dinard came on June 15 and then on the 17th they flew to the Island of Jersey. Desmond Fopp, a young Australian, then a Sergeant Pilot with 17 Squadron, remembers the move vividly:

'The CO suddenly appeared and said that all serviceable aircraft were to be flown out immediately and climbed into his aircraft for take-off. We hastily followed as he had omitted to say where to! Due to a slow start (flat battery) I remember following the last dot in the sky and eventually landed in Jersey.'

From Jersey they flew one patrol over the Cherbourg peninsula and were also scrambled once but finally on the 19th they returned to England. Most of the Hurricanes were by this time unserviceable; in fact Sergeant Fopp's machine was flown home with a burst tail wheel tyre and with no ammunition in its guns. Two pilots returned to England in a two seater Magister and two others managed to make their way back in a Fairey Battle which they had found abandoned but had been made flyable to get them home.

The weary Hurricane pilots gratefully touched down at Tangmere where after a meal and having their machines refuelled they carried on to Debden.

For the Royal Air Force, the Battle of France was over and everyone could guess what was to follow. Few people doubted that England would be next on Hitler's list. The RAF fighter losses in France had been appalling and had left Britain terribly short of the machines that really only stood between Hitler and the free world.

During the six weeks following the start of the German attacks on May 10, the Royal Air Force had lost over five hundred of its valuable and irreplaceable fighters in France and over Dunkirk. It was a time now for dramatic action and dramatic words to stir the nation to action and determination. The action was to come from the pilots of Fighter Command, the words, which summed up for everyone the position, came from the Prime Minister, Winston Churchill:

'What General Weygand called the Battle of France is over. I expect the Battle of Britain to begin. The whole fury and might of the enemy must very soon be turned on us. Hitler knows that he will have to break us in this island or lose the war. If we can stand up to him, all Europe may be free and the life of the World may move forward into broad sunlit uplands. But if we fail, then the whole World, including the United States, including all that we have known and cared for, will sink into the abyss of a new Dark Age made more sinister and perhaps more protracted, by the lights of perverted science. Let us therefore brace ourselves to our duties, and so bear ourselves that, if the British Empire and its Commonwealth last for a thousand years, men will say "This was their finest hour!" '

CHAPTER SIX

The Battle of Britain

'One crowded hour of glorious life
Is worth an age without a name.'

To many British people such phrases, as, The Battle of Britain, or The Few, mean different things. To some it is Britain standing alone against the might of Hitler's Germany, to others it is white vapour trails on a backcloth of blue summer skies, or to others it is the memory of the Blitz which was to follow.

For Flying Officer Count Manfred Czernin it was yet another great adventure, following his brief taste of action in France. He viewed this venture with some mixed feelings, for his father's native Austria was part of Hitler's empire and Italy too, the country of his youth and childhood, was now also an enemy, His mother's country, however, was also his country and his first responsibilities were to Britain and her Air Force.

There is no intention within these pages to describe in detail the great air battles waged over Southern England during the long summer of 1940, but merely to record Count Czernin's not insignificant part in it, together with that of his squadron. To those who were privileged to take part in the Battle, and those fortunate to survive, will always go the praise of the British people, and they will always be remembered. Not, however, remembered as individuals but as a Command, a unified whole. Part of the Command was number 17 Squadron, under the leadership of Squadron Leader R. I. G. MacDougall, based at RAF Debden in Fighter Command's 11 Group.

After reforming with replacement pilots and Hurricanes, 17

Squadron went back into action in July 1940. This was the period when the Luftwaffe was testing and probing Britain's defences by attacking its Channel ports and its shipping. The first clash came on July 9 for the squadron, when Ken Manger, Glyn Griffiths and Pilot Officer G. R. Bennette shot down a He111 when patrolling above convoy code named 'Agent' at 1640 hours.

At 0800 hours on July 12, 17 Squadron were ordered to provide air cover for another convoy code named 'Booty'. The squadron had moved forward from Debden to Martlesham at dawn for the day's patrols. Manfred, flying his Hurricane YB-F (V7408), led his section of A Flight out across the English coast, gaining height over the grey-green waters of the North Sea. From enemy-held territory two formations of hostile aircraft were already heading for 'Booty' – Dornier 17's and Heinkel 111's of II/KG2 and III/KG53. Radar had picked up the enemy plots and 17 Squadron were alerted to their approach. This led to more British fighters being sent up, three Hurricanes of 85 Squadron, also from Martlesham Heath, three Hurricanes from 242 Squadron at Coltishall, plus six Defiants of 264 Squadron from Duxford and 11 Hurricanes of 151 Squadron from North Weald. To Manfred, came again the tension of impending action, his blue eyes keenly searching out the grey-blue heavens for any sign of the approaching enemy bombers.

The squadron spread out into individual sections thereby covering as much an area as possible. In his rear-view mirror he could see Pilot Officer Hanson's Hurricane hovering above his own but slightly to his right, as they curved over the ships of the convoy. It was now 0848 hours.

'Bandits, three o'clock low.' It sounded like Pittman's voice, someone had seen enemy aircraft and were engaging. Manfred then spotted the Germans, 12 He111's coming in fast from the east, flying at 8,000 ft. He immediately went into a climbing turn to the left, then, stick over and a kick to the left rudder and he was plunging down to meet the bombers. Already he was firing, not accurately, just spraying the formation trying to split them up.

Pilot Officer Manger, leading Yellow Section, and his number two Sergeant Griffiths went down after one Heinkel of 8 Staffel, III/KG53 and shot it into the sea. Almost immediately, Griffiths went after a second Heinkel and this too crashed into the sea. The fight broke up. Manfred and Hanson continued through some cloud and continued to patrol above the convoy. At 0926 they saw three

Dornier 17's being harried by some other Hurricanes (151 Squadron, led by Wing Commander F. V. Beamish). Manfred and Hanson joined in, singling out one Dornier and attacking. Back with the stick, turning slightly to the right, throttle forward as he levelled out and shot after the Dornier that was already speeding low over the water towards the east. A quick look round in case of enemy fighters, but the sky was empty. Manfred gently caressed the gun button on the control column, then pressed it. The Dornier was hit. Coming in again Manfred sent another burst into the bomber. There followed several attacks from both head-on and from the stern-quarter until at last the Dornier splashed into the sea. Manfred and Hanson climbed away and headed back towards the coast then made for base.

It had been a successful morning, for in addition, Pittman and Desmond Fopp of Red Section had shot down another Heinkel. Two Dornier 17's of II/KG2 failed to return, one being Manfred's victim while 151 Squadron was credited with the other. One of the machines was piloted by Hauptmann Machetski, the unit's *Staffelkapitan*.

Manfred left for London later for a day's leave and Sergeant Fopp flew down and picked him up at Croydon in the Squadron Magister on the 14th, flying him back to Debden. For Fopp there was an interesting sequel to that trip which was rather amusing. Fopp flew to Bristol for a weekend leave and on his return was forced down by bad weather and landed on a playing field at Felsted School, only to be given a 'rocket' by the headmaster. It turned out to be none other than his old headmaster from St Peter's College, Adelaide, South Australia.

For the rest of July the squadron flew many more convoy patrols, interspersed with the occasional scramble to set the blood racing, but little action was seen. Each morning they would take off from Debden and fly to Martlesham Heath to operate from there, returning to Debden at the end of the day. On July 18 came a change of squadron commanders when Squadron Leader Cedric Williams took over from MacDougall. On the 24th Manfred and others were 'scrambled' to intercept a small raid and he went after a Junkers Ju88. He shot it up but did not see it go down and could only claim a 'damaged'.

The squadron did, however, bring down a German on the 29th, when Flight Lieutenant Alfred Bayne in company with Bird-Wilson and Pilot Officer D. H. Wissler, destroyed a He111. The three pilots intercepted the bomber over the Thames Estuary at 1530 hours and the five crewmen of III/KG55 failed to return to their French base at Villacoublay. Things appeared to be warming up, and the Luftwaffe was now ready to commence extensive air operations in an effort to eliminate the Royal Air Force so that an invasion could be mounted.

It started the first week of August and 11 Group immediately began to take the brunt of the fighting. 17 Squadron initially had to be content with patrols north of the River Thames and thereby saw little of the real fighting and were not called upon for support to the more southerly squadrons.

On the 6th, Pilot Officer H. W. A. Britton was killed during an air test, when he crashed his Hurricane in Debden Park. Two days later things really began to warm up for the pilots of Fighter Command but 17 were again to far north to be engaged. However, Manfred did lead Yellow Section off to intercept an intruder and at 1755 hours attacked a Ju88 at between 5 and 6,000 ft east of Aldeburgh. Pilot Officer Hanson (in P3539) and Pilot Officer Bennette (in N2666) saw Manfred's fire going into the Junkers but then lost it in cloud. However, the bomber was forced to jettison its bombs.

Manfred then went into hospital for a week suffering from a stomach complaint. He left on the 10th and on the 11th his squadron were scrambled and engaged several Me109's and twin engined Me110's shortly before mid-day. Luftflotten 2 and Luftflotten 3 had launched air attacks and were met by sections from six RAF squadrons, who claimed 11 of the German aeroplanes, but lost nine of their own number. 17 Squadron's own claim was two Me110's destroyed with another 'probably' destroyed. In adddition they also damaged a 109 and a 110. From this battle Ken Manger failed to return. Manger had served gallantly in France and over the Channel, having claimed seven victories. In one action on June 1 he had been shot down over Dunkirk, landing in the sea by the pier. He was picked up by a French boat, returned to England and was back in action the very next day. His was a sad loss to the squadron.

The first of several really big raids of the Battle came on August 15, but 17 Squadron did not shine that day and only one Me109 was claimed as a 'probable' by Flight Lieutenant Bill Harper. The squadron had been scrambled just after 1430 when a raid was reported making for Harwich. Only four Hurricanes got off before the raid was reported to have turned towards Martlesham. Skimming in across the aerodrome came the twin-engined

Messerschmitt 110's of Walter Rubensdorffer's Erprobungsgruppe 210, who dropped more than a score of bombs among the Station buildings, blew up a Fairey Battle, damaged the workshops and Officers' Mess. Two hangars and the watch office was badly hit and water and telephone services were disrupted, putting the aerodrome almost out of action for 48 hours. After hitting the 109, Flight Lieutenant Harper was himself shot down and forced to land at Felixstowe with wounds to his face and leg, and was taken to Felixstowe hospital.

The German unit, EG 210, attacked Croydon later that same day and suffered badly at the hand of RAF fighters. Its leader, Rubensdorffer, was shot down and killed and six others of his unit were also brought down.

Manfred returned to the squadron and was flying again on the 18th when in the morning he flew on a convoy patrol. Later in the day the squadron was scrambled twice and during one of these sorties, at 1255, they ran into about 200 enemy aircraft. Squadron Leader Williams led the attack on one formation of Dornier 17's, knocking one out of the group and seeing it go down on fire.

Suddenly a score of Messerschmitt 109's were coming down from above and everyone began to break away. One Messerschmitt fired at Manfred's Hurricane but missed, then banked away. At once Manfred was turning after it firing short bursts at the jinking enemy aeroplane. The two fighters roared over the coast, the German heading for France and safety. It began to leave a thin trail of smoke but then in his rear-view mirror Manfred spotted more 109's coming after him, so had to leave his damaged opponent some ten miles out to sea. Pushing his stick forward he dived for the deck and made his way home. Glyn Griffiths' Hurricane was damaged in the fight and he had to force land at Manston, where the machine was later destroyed in an enemy air raid. Pilot Officer N. D. Soloman was not so lucky and failed to return.

One abortive scramble and one patrol on the 19th, and then the squadron flew south to Tangmere near the Hampshire coast from where they would operate until the 26th. Tangmere, in Desmond Fopp's words: 'proved far more interesting and we were bombed on the ground on one occasion. I also remember carrying out a night patrol there and having to land back with only six blue glim lamps as a flarepath during a raid.'

The squadron was in action on the 21st, at 1715 hours. Manfred led Red Section. It was a cloudy day and the Luftwaffe resorted to small formations or just single raiders in hit-and-run raids. Red Section was sent up after a lone raider and Manfred led Squadron Leader Williams and Sergeants Bartlett and Chew in pursuit. Through scudding clouds Manfred spotted their quarry, a twin-engined Ju88 A-1. Pushing their throttles forward the four RAF fighters began to close in.

'Bandit 12 o'clock, dead ahead,' he stated briefly over the R/T and turned his guns from 'safe' to 'fire'. The German saw the four Hurricanes and began to dive for cloud. Manfred pushed forward on the stick and slowly began to overhaul the Junkers, opened fire and saw strikes hit all over the bomber. Williams too closed in and added his eight guns to the fire power. The Junkers heeled over in a sharp bank leaving a trail of smoke and then the two Sergeants took a turn at peppering the bomber. All four pilots got so close to the German that they could read plainly the code-letters on its fuselage.

'Hullo Red Section, reform, reform, he's had it,' Manfred called as he watched the enemy machine steepen its smoking dive. The Ju88 went into the sea off the Isle of Wight.

Also on the 21st, Squadron Leader Williams, leading Blue Section, with Bird-Wilson and Pilot Officer J. K. Ross, took off and shot down another Ju88 thirty minutes later. From this kill the squadron were able to salvage the swastika marking from the tail fin when the pilots visited the crash site at East Wittering. The swastika became a prized trophy.

Both of these Ju88's were from II/KG54, their pilots being Hauptmann Mainwald and Leutnant Kiefer.

Returning from his patrols and combats, Manfred always looked forward to the warm, friendly greeting he received from his pet dog Kyro. It was a beautiful elkhound who was not only his pet but also the squadron mascot. Kyro would sit for hours on the veranda of the Officers' Mess or at dispersal waiting for his master to return and, like many animals, it had that uncanny instinct to know Manfred's own aeroplane. One would have imagined that one Hurricane would seem to be much like any other but no matter how many might fly overhead before letting down towards the runway, Kyro would only jump up when Manfred's particular Hurricane came over.

One particular incident concerning Kyro even received coverage in the newspapers, when Manfred and his wife were dining at the

Mayfair Hotel one evening. The restaurant refused to provide meat for the animal and so Manfred shared his own meal with him, and this little drama was somehow picked up by a reporter whose newspaper gave it coverage. The Countess was living in a house-boat near Woodbridge where Manfred would spend his brief periods of rest during operations when based at Debden or Martlesham.

It would appear that Manfred wore, quite unofficially on one of his uniforms, tunic buttons of several Allied Air Forces, such as French, Czech, Polish and Belgium. With the foreign name of Czernin, being a count and with all those buttons, it was easy to understand why another reporter, eagerly looking for a story, assumed Manfred had served in all these various Air Forces before 'fleeing from Europe to join the ranks of the RAF.' No doubt Manfred, with his usual aplomb and tongue in cheek attitude, played the poor reporter along, for in the newspaper the next day appeared a story about Manfred which really struck a humorous vein with his pals on the squadron. The story read:

> IN FIVE FORCES
> British born Count Manfred Czernin, a relative by marriage of Dr Schuschnigg, former Austrian Chancellor, is now a Flying Officer in the RAF, serving with a Hurricane squadron. Having recently brought down his eighth Nazi aircraft, Count Czernin is spending a week's leave in London. He walked in to dinner at the Mayfair last evening accompanied by his Elkhound Cairo [sic] whose picture is painted on the side of his plane. When meat was refused Cairo, Count Czernin shared his portion with the dog.
> The airman's tunic has French, Belgium, Czech and Dutch buttons to show he has served with units of these forces.

Manfred had not as yet brought down eight enemy aircraft, but he seems to have added to his score, for the benefit of the reporter his two kills which had not been confirmed. It also sounded as if '... a week's leave in London ...' was some kind of reward for his work. The pilots of 17 Squadron knowing how Manfred liked to tell stories really went to town on poor Manfred when reading this and they concocted a reply to the newspaper. Imagine their great joy when the newspaper, taking the new information in good faith, printed it in full:

BAGGED PLANES
The adjutant and members of the RAF Squadron to which Count Czernin belongs wrote me a letter. They say:— 'In fairness to our fellow pilot we should tell you that his bag of Nazi planes up to date is eighteen not eight. He's such a modest bloke we think it our duty to let you know this. Insult from Hitler. Before the Anschluss Count Czernin owned the Czernin Palace at Vienna. Hitler wrote him and offered 30,000 R.M. for the Palace. The Count threw this insulting letter into the fire. An American had offered him £50,000 for a single picture from his gallery. Hitler has got the Czernin Palace now. It cost him nothing.

Manfred took all this leg-pulling in good part and this in turn led to a ceremonial parade where he was duly awarded the 'Line Shooter's Medal'. The Medal, about four inches in diameter and made by a silversmith was specially engraved for the occasion with, on one side a picture of Kyro's head. Squadron Leader Williams, in the presence of several grinning comrades, pinned the 'decoration' onto Manfred's tunic, on Tangmere field on August 20. It was all good clean fun although reaction had been generated by the Public Relations Officers at Air Ministry, who, after reading the newspaper article, wanted to verify the score of this 'Ace' pilot who had achieved so much without their knowledge.

Whatever some of his brother pilots might have thought of Manfred and his penchant for stretching the truth (line-shooting in RAF parlance) events in a few days' time would make them think otherwise towards him.

August 25, 1940 dawned bright and clear. It was a warm pleasant day and the pilots sat in the sun outside the dispersal area hut. The Luftwaffe was fairly quiet and 17 Squadron remained at 'readiness' as much activity was being reported from across the Channel. After standing down for lunch, the weather began to cloud over, but it continued warm. Manfred sat impatiently, smoking heavily and absent-mindedly tapping his signet ring, which he wore on the small finger of his left hand, on the wooden arm of his chair. Other pilots sprawled about in deck chairs or laid on the grass trying or pretending to doze. One or two tried to read books or magazines while trying to ignore the field telephone that at any moment might ring, and send them racing to their waiting Hurricanes.

The Hurricanes stood silently only a few paces away, the mechanics, on whom so much depended, sitting idly in little groups under the broad wings of the aircraft or stretched out in the sun. All was quiet and the war seemed very far away. A Lysander flew slowly across the far horizon, the noise of its engine hardly perceptible above the chirruping of the birds in the nearby trees.

Towards tea-time a raid of 50+ bandits was plotted near St Malo and was tracked by the radar operators as flying towards Cherbourg where it joined up with other plots that were the escorting fighters. These plots swelled the raid to an estimated 100+. Off the Channel Islands another plot of 30+ began to build up gradually until it too was estimated at 100+, to the operators' experienced eyes. In Fighter Command's 11 Group Headquarters Operations Room, the enemy plots could be seen beginning to head in the general direction of Weymouth. Could this be yet another feint by the Luftwaffe, hoping to draw the RAF fighters up into the air, only to turn and frustrate the defenders? No, this seemed to be a definite raid. Telephones began to ring.

'Scramble,' yelled Williams, '100+ heading for Weymouth.' Suddenly everyone was running towards their Hurricanes. The ground crews were already starting them up and the quiet of the late afternoon was shattered by the healthy roar of Rolls Royce Merlin engines. It was 17.45 pm.

Manfred reached his 'F', pulled the parachute from the wing onto his back and helped by one of his mechanics, locked the straps to the central release box. Climbing up, he dropped down into the cockpit, the parachute pack fitting into the aluminium bucket seat. Already he was waving away the chocks, then after strapping himself in and pulling on his flying helmet he began to taxi the machine forward, his experienced eyes running over the instrument panel. Gauges, engine temperature, revs; oil pressure, boost, radiator shutter lever pulled back ...

Already Williams was leaving the ground, as Manfred gave the machine full throttle and began to race across the bumpy green grass of the aerodrome. The Hurricane lifted into the air and Manfred subconsciously checked the aircraft to himself: 'Ease back the stick, back a bit on the boost – mustn't overstrain. Close the cockpit hood and retract the undercarriage – red lights showing ... now green ... good. Flip the red handle on the right of the instrument panel to

The Avro Tutor, used by No. 6 Flying Training School, Netheravon, and the type on which Manfred learned to fly.

Hawker Hind day bomber flown by 83 Squadron. In this machine (K6636) Manfred took part in the Royal Escort on July 28, 1937. K6636 was destroyed in a crash in August 1938 after Manfred had left the Squadron.

Blackburn B2 (G-ADLG). Flown by Manfred in August 1939 while attending an Instructors Course at Hanworth, with the RAF. The Course was terminated by the declaration of War.

(Far left) The Mayfair Playboy and 'Man about Town'.

(Left) On active service from the first day of war, Manfred, September 1939.

(Right) May 1940. Some of Manfred's comrades in 85 Squadron, France. From left to right: F/Lt J R M Boothby, S/Ldr J O W Oliver DSO DFC, Fg Off J Leckie, Fg Off K H Blair and Sgt G Allard DFM. This picture was taken on the day the Blitzkrieg began, May 10, after these five pilots had returned from shooting down 7 German aeroplanes.

(Left) With Maud Hamilton. It was love at first sight and they were married in November 1939. The fighter pilot and the debutante.

ight) Hawker Hurricanes 85 Squadron, France, 1940

Awaiting the Battle. Members of A Flight, 17 Squadron at Debden, July 1940. From left to right: Fg Off D Hanson, F/Lt W J Harper, Plt Off G R Bennette, Fg Off L W Stevens, Fg Off G E Pittman and Sgt G Griffiths.

Flying Officer L W Stevens taxies out YB-J (N2359) of 17 Squadron during the Battle of Britain. It carries a picture of 'Popeye' on the fuselage and Manfred's Hurricane carried a picture of his dog 'Kyro'.

raise the flaps, push back the black knob on the cockpit floor to close the coolant shutters ....'

The sections were forming up, still climbing hard. Manfred checked his R/T, calling up his section. 'Check Yellow Section.'

'Yellow Two.'

'Yellow Three.'

All OK and the radio working satisfactorily – the other sections checked in to their respective leaders. 10,000 feet already and still climbing. Still rather cloudy but visibility good although hazy towards the horizon. The sea looked blue and not uninviting below and the Isle of Wight was now slipping below the trailing edges of their wings. 14,000 feet – still gaining height, must keep a good look out. It was getting warm under the perspex cockpit canopies. 18,000 feet now and the squadron was just south-east of Portland Bill.

'Hullo Leader, hullo Leader, bandits ten o'clock above.'

All eyes were peering ahead and to the left; yes, there they were, Me109's and Me110's. Williams gave rapid orders to his sections but already a formation of 15 to 20 twin-engined 110's were almost upon them.

The Hurricanes were still climbing steeply towards the Messerschmitts, full throttle and in line astern. To the last man. Sergeant Leonard Bartlett, flying Hurricane P3673, hovering on the stall, it seemed in itself a stupid manoeuvre, for the Hurricanes would have little flying speed left to be able to do much then the two formations met. Sergeant Bartlett, now Group Captain, DSO, RAF Retired, relates:

'My concern didn't lessen when they (the 110's) broke straight at us. I can't really remember what happened from then on, except that the sky seemed full of flaming aircraft, they were 110's being shot down by Manfred. I think he got three before the rest broke off and went home, with us in hot pursuit.'

As the 110's came down Squadron Leader Williams (flying R4199) took on the first in a head-on attack. Bartlett continues:

'The CO got another, although he went down in the attack. I was with both of them (Williams and Manfred) and it really was quite an experience. Firstly watching the two aircraft flying towards each other, head-on and both firing hard. At about 400 yards they both appeared to stop in mid-flight and flutter gently to pieces. I then joined up with three other Hurricanes – led by Manfred who proceeded to do the same thing towards the circling 110's.'

Manfred went after a 110 that broke away from its dive, and fired at it from above head-on. It nosed down and burst into flames, crashing into the sea below. Climbing up to resume the attack Manfred half rolled, dived on another Messerschmitt that turned away pouring out smoke and it too dived down vertically, burst into flames and crashed into the sea.

Manfred was then attacked by a friendly Spitfire but its pilot was a bad shot and its fire missed the Hurricane. Manfred managed to shake him off, then he went after a third 110. The Messerschmitt dropped under the British pilot's accurate fire and began to lose height, being then attacked by another Hurricane. With both of its engines stopped, the doomed 110 was then attacked by two Spitfires from 609 Squadron, flown by Squadron Leader C. Darley and Flight Lieutenant J. H. G. McArthur, who followed it down until it crashed into a wood near Warmwell aerodrome and exploded, taking its crew, Leutnant Westphal and Obergefreite Josef Brief to their death.

Apart from the loss of its gallant Commanding Officer, it had been a great day for the squadron. A total of five Me110's had been destroyed and three more sufficiently damaged to claim as 'probables'. Three Me109's had also been accounted for with another two as "probables".

The raid had been mounted by various Luftwaffe units, comprising Ju88's of II/KG51 escorted by Me110's from I/ZG2 and Me109's from I and II Gruppen of JG53. They had been engaged by 17, 87, 152, 213, 602 and 609 Squadrons. The first two 110's which Manfred had shot down came from I/ZG2 while the third which he shared with Darley and McArthur also came from this unit. I/ZG2 lost a total of five 110's, the number claimed by 17 Squadron, and JG/53 lost three 109's and had two other pilots wounded. Arthur Bayne, after shooting down a 109 of JG/53 was hit from fire from another just south of Tangmere. He baled out and was rescued from the sea unhurt.

This action, along with his other previous exploits, gained for Manfred the award of the Distinguished Flying Cross, which was officially Gazetted on October 1, 1940, the actual announcement being made by their Station Commander on September 11.

News of his award was mentioned in the daily papers and it is still evident that the story of his service with 'other air forces' was still thought to be correct. The story was accompanied by a photograph of Manfred and Maud.

IN FIVE AIR FORCES: WINS THE DFC
Count Manfred Czernin (seen dancing with the Countess) has been awarded the DFC. He led his section in head-on attack against large formations of enemy (planes) and himself destroyed three planes. Born in Berlin in 1913, the Count wears on his tunic, buttons of the French, Czech, Polish and Belgian Air Forces with which he has gone into action.'

After the action above Portland Bill on the 25th, Manfred's score of victories was beginning to be impressive without any need for line shooting to be written.

On the evening of the 25th, after a later but uneventful patrol, Manfred flew his first night-fighter patrol, without success and, like Desmond Fopp, had to land back during a raid. The following day 17 Squadron left Tangmere for Northolt, where during the next four days they were scrambled several times but only claimed a 'probable' Me110, attacked by Alfred Bayne, on the 27th. They were more successful on the 31st, when Bird-Wilson shot down an Me109 flown by Oberleutnant von Perthes of I/LG2, while Bayne claimed another. Bird-Wilson also shot pieces off a third but could only claim a 'damaged'. On September 2, the squadron returned to Debden, but by this date a new CO had been appointed, Squadron Leader A. G. Miller who came from the Fighter Interception Unit at Tangmere.

The morning of September 3, the war's first anniversary, again found the pilots of 17 Squadron at 'readiness'. It was another warm day, but then every day seemed long, warm and sunny during that summer. The boys lounged about at dispersal, Manfred smoking leisurely, watching the smoke curl upwards in the still air. It was amazing to look back over the previous twelve months; so much had happened.

On the other side of the Channel, the aircraft of Luftflotten 2, scattered at various bases in Holland, Belgium and Northern France were preparing for another day of air attacks against the British Isles. Apart from dress, language, background and of course ideologies, the German pilots and aircrew differed but slightly from their opponents now waiting for them in Southern England. All enjoyed the thrill and adventure of flying and the freedom only to be found in the skies, although they all knew how, in war, death or glory waited hand in hand in their silent blue world. The Grim Reaper waited to cut down the slow or unwary.

Soon after eight o'clock, the now familiar build-up of enemy aircraft was reported over Calais and the Belgium border by British radar. Fighter Command Headquarters became a hive of activity and expectancy. The Lion reared its head and sniffed the air!

For the German Eagle, the targets were known; the airfields of the RAF at Hornchurch, North Weald and – Debden!

At 1025 hours the shrill ring of the telephone sent the pilots running to their fighters and once in the air 17 Squadron formed up and were advised that it was likely to be their own backyard that they would be defending. The sections were soon gaining as much height as possible and Manfred in his 'F' watched as his section kept station behind him. Then they saw them. A huge, awe inspiring mass of aircraft that seemed to fill the whole sky – an estimated 150 to 200 German aeroplanes, mostly Dornier bombers with escorting Messerschmitts.

Royal Air Force fighters joined combat some distance from the enemy's intended target and in a series of somewhat disjointed dog-fights, the armada began to be split up. 17 Squadron went after one group of Dorniers over the Crouch Estuary, belonging to II/KG2 whose target was North Weald. The bombers were being closely escorted by Me110's of I/ZG2 and II/ZG26.

Flight Lieutenant Bayne and his section hammered one Dornier, sending it down on fire then they turned to attack a 110, destroying this also. Harold Bird-Wilson, Ross and Sergeant D. A. Sewell accounted for another Dornier while Pilot Officer Hanson got yet another, which crashed into the River Crouch. Hanson, however, was in trouble. Hit by return fire from the Dornier his Hurricane (P3539) began to go down. Hanson struggled to get out, but by the time he did so he was down to 100 feet. He baled out but his parachute had not the time to operate and he hit the ground at almost the same moment as his machine which crashed on Foulness Island.

Manfred, meantime, led his section, Sergeant Fopp and Pilot Officer Geoff Pittman, head-on into a formation of 40 Dorniers and two formations of twin-engined Messerschmitts but with no visible results. Speeding past and through the enemy formation, a 110 turned after Manfred and began to open fire from the beam. Manfred kicked out at his rudder and screamed into a tight turn, hauled the Hurricane round after his antagonist and as the 110 came into his sights, fired again with two quick bursts from his eight machine guns. The 110 went straight down, burst into flames, hit the ground and exploded. Manfred was already after a second Messerschmitt, firing as he closed in. This 110 nosed over and dived vertically but Manfred lost sight of it when he went down behind three more enemy aircraft, but they turned out to be friendly Blenheims. His second 110, however, was later confirmed when the wreck was found in a wood two miles north of Maldon. This was also claimed by Sub-Lieutenant J. C. Carpenter, a Navy pilot attached to 46 Squadron, and was flown by Leutnant Manhard and Unteroffizier Drewes. Carpenter was in fact killed five days later.

Manfred's first victim was believed to be a machine from I/ZG2 for this unit lost two 110's although both crews baled out, a fact that Manfred did not mention in his report of the action. Another 110 of 6/ZG26 was badly hit in this fight and its gunner, Unteroffizier Klatt, baled out but his pilot managed to fly his crippled machine back to France but crashed near Fontend. This is more probably the second machine which Manfred hit and as it was a virtual write-off after its crash a second victory can be substantiated.

Desmond Fopp, flying as Manfred's number two, records this memory of the fight. He was not flying his usual machine YB-I but YB-E (P3673), a Hurricane which had had three inches cut off the propeller blades following a taxiing accident. Fopp had reason to remember this particular combat:

'The attack on the forty Ea head-on I remember only two well! We were scrambled rather late and did not get sufficient altitude to achieve a favourable attacking position from above, with the result that we had to attack head-on at about 20,000 feet and hope to break up the large formation of Do17's with guns blazing which did separate them considerably. We then turned back to attack individually and of course in the melee which occurred I lost contact with the Count.

'I had just put a Do17 engine out and he was smoking badly when I saw three Me110's coming in behind from a long line astern. By this time I had run out of ammunition but decided that as I could not match them for speed I would turn into them and simulate an attack. This I did and to my astonishment and joy they broke all round me so I immediately half rolled and dived for the deck. Unfortunately for me one of them was also below and behind out of sight and managed to put a cannon shell into my radiator, with the result that all I heard was a thump and the next second I was sitting in a ball of fire.

'Having recovered from the shock my next move was to get out and away from the fire – this I managed at my second attempt as I first tried to get out with my straps still on. My relief on getting away from the flames was so great that I almost forgot to pull the ripcord which caused an inadvertent delayed drop for several thousand feet and got me clear of the other aircraft which was probably a good thing.

'I then drifted down feeling glad to be alive and frantically putting out the fires which were still smouldering on my tunic and trousers. I came down in a wood and went straight through the trees without any serious damage and finished up with my toes touching the ground. I released my harness which was still smouldering and staggered out of the wood almost blind to be greeted by a couple of farm labourers armed with pitchforks who would have quite happily set about me as I was unrecognisable but my language was such that they were quickly convinced that I was British. Some kindly old lady tore strips off her petticoat to cover my burns until an ambulance arrived and took me to Brentwood Hospital where I remained for three months.'

Altogether, the squadron claimed three Dorniers and five Messerschmitts plus another 'probably' destroyed. More important, however, was the fact that the Germans had not got through to all their targets, and only North Weald was bombed. In the air, honours were even, for 16 RAF fighters had been lost with eight pilots saved, while a total of enemy machines lost was roughly the same. In addition to Hanson's loss and Desmond Fopp being wounded Squadron Leader Miller had been shot up and his Hurricane damaged by a 110 but he had successfully force-landed near North Weald.

Manfred's personal score of victories had now reached ten confirmed destroyed, plus two others shared.

The squadron's next action came on the 5th. As on previous days the Luftwaffe divided its main thrust in two major attacks, each formation making for its designated target after reaching the English coast, in a hope to confuse the defenders.

The first raids of the day came at 1000 am, enemy groups making for the aerodromes of Croydon, Biggin Hill and Eastchurch. Another raid made for North Weald and 17 Squadron scrambled but made no contact.

After a hurried sandwich and tea dinner the squadron were again at 'readiness' when another aid was reported at 1500 hours, and they were scrambled a few minutes later. The enemy raid consisted of He111's of 7/KG53 escorted by Me109's of III/JG54, briefed to attack the oil tanks at Thameshaven. Manfred, leading Yellow section, sighted 15 He111's and about 30 Messerschmitts flying west near Chatham. Squadron Leader Miller led his pilots into the attack near Gravesend while Hurricanes of 303 Squadron engaged some of the 109's.

Manfred and Sergeant Glyn Griffiths made a beam attack on the last vic of bombers, while Yellow Three – Sergeant Chew, kept a look-out behind for the 109's flying above. Closing in on one Heinkel, Manfred fired two bursts at it and flames spurted from its starboard engine. It began to lose height but Manfred left it to support Griffiths who was finishing off another bomber, but, like Manfred, he could later only report a claim for a 'probable'. However, Manfred's fire on the first bomber had found their mark and the machine, badly crippled, lost more height with its engine still on fire. It was then fired on by Pilot Officer Eric Lock of 41 Squadron and finally the German ditched and sank just off the Nore. One crew member was killed but three others survived as prisoners, reporting that they thought they had been hit by AA fire.

Manfred and Sergeant Chew, meantime, had closed with another Heinkel. Both opened fire and the bomber nosed over and crashed near Chatham. Two of the crew took to their parachutes but only one functioned properly and Feldwebel Bohn came down in the sea. His body was washed ashore at Reculver four weeks later.

By this time several 109's were coming down and Manfred's section was attacked by one from behind. Manfred throttled back and went into a tight turn, coming round, diving behind the 109 who had overshot him. Manfred kept above the Messerschmitt and when the German pilot began to climb from his dive, he fired a long accurate burst from his guns. The 109 reared up, stalled, flopped down and dived earthwards. The enemy pilot, Feldwebel Dettler of 9 Staffel JG54, baled out but his parachute too failed to open and he fell to his death on Pitsea Marshes where his body remained undiscovered for twelve days. His aeroplane crashed on a farm at South Benfleet.

Flight Lieutenant Alfred Bayne also engaged a 109 which was flown by the Gruppen Kommander of III/JG54, Hauptmann Fritz Ultsch. The 109 went down under Bayne's fire and crashed at Bowers Gifford, killing its pilot.

Manfred landed back at Debden one hour and ten minutes after take-off, to find most of the others already back. Apart from Manfred's and Bayne's claims, three other Heinkels had been left in various states of disrepair and were claimed as 'probables'.

Although over the next few days Fighter Command had no respite from air engagements, 17 Squadron saw no further action until September 11. They were, however, scrambled twice on the 6th and again on the 7th, the day Luftwaffe bombers first strayed over Britain's capital, dropping bombs on the city. This led, following a retaliatory raid on Berlin by Bomber Command, to Hitler switching his attacks from RAF airfields to the city itself. While this was bad news for the civilian population it came none too soon for Fighter Command's hard-pressed aerodromes.

On the 7th, Manfred was asked to sit for a portrait sketch by Captain Cuthbert Orde, who had been commissioned by the Air Ministry to make several studies of some of the Service's personalities. Looking at the drawing today one cannot detect the strain that was put daily upon Manfred and his fellow pilots, but there seems to be that somewhat defiant, head-erect and clear-eyed fortitude that sustained them all during that hectic summer of 1940.

The hectic summer continued for 17 Squadron on the 11th. Following a convoy patrol in the morning, they were 'scrambled' in the afternoon and ran into about 15 Me110's. Manfred, again leading Yellow section destroyed one and Alfred Bayne claimed another. These two 110's were from ZG26, whose II Gruppe lost three of their machines piloted by Oberleutnant Walter Henken of Stab/II ZG26, (Manfred's victim), Oberleutnant Randonald Birkner, (shot down by 73 Squadron), and Leutnant Rudolf Volk of 6/ZG26 (Bayne's victim). II and III Gruppen of Zerstorergeschwager 26, had taken off for London at 1540 pm German time, but these three pilots and their crewmen, plus another machine from III Gruppe (also shot down by 73 Squadron) never returned to their French bases at Crecy-en-Ponthieu, Barley and Arques. The body of Feldwebel Radelmeier, the rear gunner of Manfred's victim, was washed ashore at Margate on October 23.

17 Squadron's only casualty during the fight was Sergeant Bartlett, whose Hurricane was shot up by one of the 110's but he managed to land safely back at base.

On Sunday September 15, the day that forever will be known as

'Battle of Britain Day', 17 Squadron was one of the few front line units not to claim any real successes against the huge air effort mounted by the Luftwaffe. The remarks in Manfred's log-book probably sums up the reason:

> Scramble – attacked enormous Balbo but could get no conclusive results.

They were in the air for ninety minutes but only Bird-Wilson and Pilot Officer Stevens were able to make any claims. They both damaged Dornier 17's of KG2, Pilot Officer P. Niemic, a Polish pilot, later damaged another.

Again there came a period of unsuccessful and wearying scrambles by the squadron during the 16th, 17th and 18th and not once were they able to make any encounters with the enemy. Just after 1500 hours on the 17th, Flight Lieutenant Bayne had the engine of his Hurricane suddenly cut out when taking off from Debden and had to make a rapid forced-landing. The machine was destroyed in the crash but Bayne walked away unhurt. The next day two Hurricanes were damaged following a minor mid-air collision between Squadron Leader Tony Miller and Leonard Bartlett.

Manfred, leading Red section for a change, was scrambled on the 19th shortly before 1100 hours. It was a showery day with very little enemy activity, except for single aeroplanes on nuisance or reconnaissance missions. Climbing above cloud, control vectored Manfred and his two companions, Sergeants Bartlett (in V7241) and Griffiths (V6553) YB-J, onto a hostile plot approaching a convoy in the North Sea. Through scudding clouds they finally sighted a Ju88 flying north at 14,000 ft. It was about ten miles from them when Manfred radioed the 'Tally-ho' to control, confirming contact with the enemy machine, and began the chase.

There seemed little hope of catching it before they lost it in cloud but then without reason the Junkers suddenly turned, changed course and flew straight towards the three Hurricanes. Its crew had obviously not seen the British fighters but it soon did so and began to dive.

Manfred led an attack from the beam and from underneath, giving the German's port engine a three-second burst. Thick smoke spewed back from the engine which promptly stopped. Glyn Griffiths then attacked followed by Bartlett. They left the German with both its engines on fire and going down. Manfred closed in again from the beam and the bomber went into a glide. Griffiths closed again and fired then followed by the three Hurricanes the Junkers went into the grey waters of the sea some ten miles off the British coast.

Some records indicate that the machine was from 4(F)/121 flown by Leutnant Helmut Knab but he crashed on Oakington aerodrome at 1500 hours, some four hours later! 17 Squadron's victim was most probably from 1/KGr 806, a German Naval reconnaissance unit, who lost Oberfeldwebel Sowade and his crew on this date. Twenty-two years old Glyn Griffiths was more than happy to be safely back at base for he hadn't wanted to fly at all on the 19th. The reason was simple. He had just been granted a 48 hour leave pass to get married, but he was soon away and happily married the next day.

On the 21st, Manfred flew to Northolt aerodrome, returning the following day, 'in lousy weather, via a field!' His next two log-book entries read:

23rd Sept. scrambled twice – no contact.
24th Sept. scrambled on four occasions.

During the first of these four sorties of September 24, they ran into several Me109's. It was a hazy sort of day and the 109's, were not keen to 'mix it' with the Hurricanes. Later that day they were ordered off to intercept a mixed formation of Dornier 17 and Dornier 215 bombers together with Heinkel 111's, escorted by Me109's, their target being London. 17 Squadron acted as rearguard to 73 Squadron but were bounced by German fighters.

Twenty years old Harold Bird-Wilson, DFC, was hit by fire from a 109. There was a terrific explosion in his cockpit followed by fire spreading from the damaged fuel tank in front of him. 'Birdy' was severely wounded but managed to get out of his blazing machine and his parachute was escorted down out of the combat area by Manfred, Glyn Griffiths and Stevens who circled about him. He finally splashed down into the River Thames. Pilot Officer D. H. Wissler was hit by another 109, crashed on trying to land back at base and was slightly injured.

As some slight recompence for their wounded pride, Manfred attacked one Messerschmitt and saw it go down off Margate. He was credited with a 'probable' but it would appear that the German got home. Pilot Officer G. E. Pittman also claimed a 109 'damaged'.

17 Squadron were not called upon during the 25th and 26th as activity by the Luftwaffe was restricted to the Bristol area and parts of the south-west coast. The unit took the time to put in some flying practice, or so it appears when reading Manfred's log-book, but the exact nature of the flights can only be a matter of conjecture when one reads his brief entries:

25th Led a pansy flight formation.
26th scramble – Tally-hoed on Red 2 and forced Anson to land.

Things became more serious the following day when heavy attacks on London were resumed. The enemy machines consisted of bomb-carrying Me110's escorted by single-seat 109's. The enemy groups were attacked continually by Spitfires and Hurricanes all the way from Dungeness right up to the outskirts of London. 17 Squadron were scrambled at 0905 am and with 73 Squadron met a huge formation of about 30 Me110's flying in a vast circle over Redhill. To Sergeant Glyn Griffiths it seemed as if everyone was suddenly diving at the circle, flying around it or inside it, firing into any 110 that presented itself briefly in their gun-sights. After the fight the pilots made the following claims:

F/O M. B. Czernin	1 Me110 destroyed
P/O D. C. Leary	1 Me110 destroyed, 1 Me110 Probable
Sgt G. A. Steward	1 Me110 destroyed
Sgt R. D. Hogg	1 Me110 destroyed
Sgt G. Griffiths	1 Me110 destroyed, 1 Me110 Probable

The Me110's were from V/LG1; Manfred claimed his opponent crashing and exploding on the ground east of Redhill. This later proved to be incorrect as far as the locality was concerned but this can easily happen in the heat of combat. Most of LG1's losses crashed further south or west. There was certainly some very confused fighting, and at least eight 110's were brought down during this fight, claimed by 17, 72 and 46 Squadrons and another crash-landed near Dieppe after being hit in combat with RAF fighters.

Sergeant Hogg was one of a gaggle of British fighters to chase

Oberleutnant von Grafenreuth, Kapitan of 15/LG1. The 110 he was flying was harried some distance by both Hurricanes and Spitfires, including Manfred, and when it finally blundered over Gatwick aerodrome was hit again by the station defences. It exploded on impact killing the Kapitan and his rear man Feldwebel Reinhold.

Later that day Glyn Griffiths brought down a Messerschmitt 109 from 6/JG3, the machine going into the sea, the pilot being rescued by the German *Seenotflugkommando*. However, Griffiths' main recollection of that day was of chasing a Ju88 but he spun in cloud and lost it and landed at Detling. To him, that September day, there seemed to be thousands of German aircraft in the air and some of the squadron's combats that day were very high for Hurricanes, up to 27,000 ft.

Manfred did in fact chase three other 110's back as far as the French coast, before having to break off the combat. The Germans as a whole had been badly mauled over London and were forced to split up and head for home, at ground level in many cases.

On this day the Luftwaffe lost a total of 55 aircraft, which made it the third-best day for the RAF fighters. On August 15 the RAF had claimed 75 raiders brought down and on September 15 a total of 60 had been accounted for.

Air activity in terms of combat became greatly reduced for 17 Squadron from the beginning of, and throughout, October, although a high number of operational sorties were flown. Fighter squadrons farther south still felt the whole weight of the Luftwaffe's remaining attempts but even here they were reduced to hit-and-run raids, mostly flown by Me109 and Me110 machines now relegated to a fighter-bomber role.

On October 2, Flight Lieutenant Bayne took off with Pilot Officer H. P. 'Cowboy' Blatchford, J. K. Ross and Flying Officer F. Fajtl to intercept a Dornier 17z of Stab/KG2, flown in fact by the Staffel Kapitan Oberleutnant Hans Langer. It was a long chase but finally they overtook the German and sent it down near Pulham, South Norfolk, where Langer and his crew were taken prisoner. Blatchford and Fajtl both had to force-land near Pulham through lack of fuel.

17 Squadron left Debden on October 8 and began to operate from Martlesham Heath, where it shared the aerodrome with 257 Squadron, under the command of one of the most famous RAF fighter-pilots, Squadron Leader Robert Stanford Tuck. For the next

four days the squadron also used Hornchurch during the day, were scrambled more than a dozen times but failed to make any contact.

Pilot Officer Ross had an unpleasant experience on the 13th; when flying over Chatham, he was hit by friendly AA fire, which forced him to take to his parachute.

After lunch on the 14th, Manfred and Pilot Officer Pittman were on stand-by but with little real hope of action owing to extremely bad weather conditions. For most of the day it had been dull and overcast with rain and drizzle limiting visibility considerably. At twenty minutes past two an unidentified aircraft was picked up on the radar screens and shortly after two-thirty, Control ordered Czernin and Pittman to take off and investigate this assumedly hostile plot. In ten-tenths cloud they climbed up and away from Martlesham and were vectored towards the intruder.

Manfred spotted an aircraft flying west and fired a warning burst of fire across its nose as he could see RAF markings on the wings. The aircraft replied with flares coloured 'Red-Red', which were not the colours of the day, but as Manfred identified the machine as a Blenheim, broke away. Flying through dense cloud formations they then spotted in occasional breaks what appeared to be a lone Dornier 17 flying south. Again the two British pilots were in something of a dilemma, for the Dornier also carried British markings on the upper surfaces of the wings and on the tail rudders. The two Hurricanes closed in like two sniffing hounds when the Dornier's crew saw them and turned sharply away.

As it banked round Manfred saw the familiar black German crosses on the undersides of the wings. Immediately he was turning tightly after it, firing his eight guns, his bullets smashing into the starboard wing and engine. Fire broke out in the engine and the Ea dived into cloud. Manfred was unable to follow as his instruments were not functioning properly but Pittman (in P3623) closed in to give the German several bursts as they flew in and out of cloud but Pittman finally had to leave the enemy when the German pilot, with some courage, made his escape by flying right through the Harwich balloon barrage.

This Dornier was probably from 1/NJG2, which was making an intruder sortie over Suffolk on this day. The machine reached its base but three of its crew had been wounded. It would also seem certain that this was the same machine that Manfred first encountered and which he thought was a Bristol Blenheim.

The following day the squadron provided air cover over a British convoy but Manfred and the others were fired on by the trigger-happy sailors who could not really be blamed for their 'shoot-first' policy although a few unfriendly words were undoubtedly directed at the seamen.

Following another busy but non-active period, Manfred and his section were ordered off after a lone Dornier on October 24, flying a lone reconnaissance mission. The enemy, proving to be a Dornier 215, had crossed the English coast at Southwold in Suffolk and had penetrated as far as the Midlands. With Manfred was Sergeant Hogg and Pilot Officer Fajtl.

The section was vectored into position whereby they would be able to intercept the bomber on its return flight. Flying in difficult weather conditions Manfred waited for his prey which at this very moment was being attacked by a section of Hurricanes of 1 Squadron who inflicted some damage on the Dornier.

Then Manfred spotted the Dornier, on its own, coming through cloud and turned his section into an attacking position. He flipped the gunsight switch and the orange-coloured circle of light appeared in the middle of the sighting glass on the sight, which represented a 100 mph in deflection shots. He had already adjusted the two bars on the glass, which could be widened or closed depending on the wing span of the enemy. When he had taken off he knew he would be up against a twin-engined bombing type machine and had adjusted the sight accordingly.

Carefully he turned the guns switch from 'safe' to 'fire'. He was now closing fast, 400 yards, – 300 yards, – his guns were harmonized for 200 yards and at this distance he thumbed the gun button on the control column. The familiar shuddering occurred as his eight machine-guns sent a stream of bullets into the enemy. Almost at once the Dornier began to leave a trail of smoke and Manfred fired again then broke away. His two companions then attacked, both giving the enemy a burst of fire. The Dornier, now well alight, began to lose height rapidly and two parachutes appeared before the Dornier crashed at the Bell Inn, Eaton Socon, near St Neots, Huntingdonshire. 17 Squadron's sortie had lasted sixty minutes.

1 Squadron's Hurricanes also made the claim for the Dornier's destruction but the sole German survivor Obergefreite Max Dorr, confirmed that it had been 17 Squadron's attacks that had done the major damage and brought them down. The Dornier was from

3/Aufkl.Gr.Ob.d.L. (3rd Staffel of *Aufklarungsgruppe Oberbefehlshaber Der Luftwaffe*) a reconnaissance unit, and had been engaged on a photo-reconnaissance sortie of Coventry and Birmingham.

On the 27th, Martlesham aerodrome was attacked at 1640 pm by a number of bomb-carrying Me109's, an attack carried out simultaneously with two others on both Southampton and London. As the alarm sounded, Manfred raced to the nearest Hurricane and without even taking time to strap on a parachute, took off just as the first bombs fell. Climbing steeply and trying to avoid the incoming fighters he gained some height before turning to pursue one of the Messerschmitts. He closed briefly and opened fire but without any apparent results and he finally lost the 109 in cloud.

He landed again at 5 o'clock and was off again twenty minutes later in company with Pilot Officer Ross, this time to intercept another raid reported coming in across the coast. They became separated and Ross found a Dornier 17 which he attacked as the German made for cloud cover. Ross got off only a short burst but observed no result. Later, however, this machine was seen to crash in the River Stour, the Dornier coming from III/KG76.

Manfred's next combats came the next day, and were the last in his favourite 'F' for some time. In the morning single raiders came over during this rather cloudy day and he took off in company with Leonard Bartlett at 0735 and intercepted a Dornier 215 ten miles off Orfordness. After each pilot had made three attacks they broke off the action when the Dornier was down to 1,500 ft, losing height and with its starboard engine on fire. They landed at 0845 but could only claim a damaged. A Dornier from I/KG3 was shot down in the area that day and it was thought to be their victim until it was confirmed that the Ea was shot down by AA fire at 1300 hours.

Manfred now took over Hurricane YB-J (V6553) previously flown by Griffiths and had to spend some time adjusting it to his own particular requirements. These adjustments included the harmonization of the guns, setting the gun sight and adjusting rudder pedals, the latter item being of some importance to his tall frame (6ft, 1½ ins).

His first and only combat in 'J' took place on October 30, during his fourth sortie of the day. The Luftwaffe again occupied itself in fighter sweeps and fighter-bomber attacks, dispatching several raids during the day. In the afternoon Manfred checked for the fourth time his machine, chatted with his ground crew and formally signed the

Form 700, accepting the Hurricane from their dutiful care and attention.

He was strolling back to the dispersal hut when the scramble came. As the others came crashing from the hut, Manfred was already fitting on his parachute and then climbed into the cockpit. Straps fastened, he took the soft leather flying helmet from its resting place on the gun-sight and pulled it onto his head. He then pushed the oxygen supply nozzle on the end of the black hose from his face mask, into the oxygen supply outlet, turning the nozzle to lock it in place. This was followed by plugging the lead wire from the helmet into a radio wire connection on the right-hand side of the cockpit floor. This completed he quickly went through the pre-take-off checks and was then away.

All these actions had taken only seconds, done in the main without any real thought, being reflex actions carried out every time he took to the air. It had only taken a few brief moments from clambering into the cockpit to the moment when the breaks were released and the Hurricane was gathering speed across the grass of the aerodrome. Manfred pushed forward on the throttle lever and began to gather speed, easing back on the boost as the machine lifted from the ground.

The squadron flew in sections of two over the Maidstone area at 25,000 ft. Flying through large cloud formations, Manfred spotted a large gaggle of 20 to 30 Me109's south-west of him and about 1,000 ft above. He then saw two more 109's below at 18,000 ft. Making sure no other enemy fighters were in the immediate vicinity, above or behind, he dived down after them. Coming down out of the sun he closed in on the rearmost machine only to discover that it was a Hurricane. The leading machine was, however, a Messerschmitt, so he closed right in and gave it a burst from his guns from astern and above. The 109 dived immediately then began to climb. Manfred followed and fired again from 250 yards keeping his thumb on the button until he was only 20 yards from his opponent. The 109 literally flew through his fire and was hit from nose to tail. The German stalled, turned over onto its back and went straight down, pouring out black smoke, to disappear into cloud at about 5,000 ft.

Manfred could only put in a claim for a 'possible' but the wreckage was found and it was therefore raised to a 'confirmed destroyed' victory, and his combat report was endorsed accordingly. However, this claim is in doubt, for Flying Officer R. C. Dafforn and

Sergeant J. H. Lacey of 504 Squadron flying in the same area, attacked a 109 and blew its wing off. The pilot, Unteroffizier Alfred Fahrain, baled out and his machine exploded on the ground. Pilot Officer A. F. Eckford of 253 Squadron also claimed a 109 shot down and like Manfred saw it go down into cloud and, as he broke through cloud himself, saw a 109 burning on the ground.

One Me109 from 4/JG3 was severely damaged but the pilot coaxed his machine home only to crash-land at Wissant. This may well have been Manfred's victim, although it is recorded that at least two other 109's from other units also returned to France badly shot up. It is also possible that the Hurricane Manfred saw initially was either Dafforn or Lacey who may have made their attack after Manfred had hit the 109, but the true facts will probably never be known.

Glyn Griffiths was the only other pilot to claim a Messerschmitt 109, the pilot, Unteroffizier Eugen Schuller also taking to his parachute. These 109's from JG/3 'Udet' came from the Pas de Calais area and had been escorting other JG3 109's carrying bombs. Griffith's award of the DFM was announced on November 13.

Two days and two patrols later, Manfred went on leave, and was later to regret this departure, for on November 8 the squadron had one of its most successful days since the height of the Battle.

It was Friday afternoon. The pilots were due to leave dispersal and go over to their messes for tea but they decided to stay and arranged for tea to be brought over. Flight Lieutenant Bayne, in temporary command of the squadron, later admitted that they '... all seemed to have a hunch something was going to happen.'

Before the tea arrived they were scrambled, at 1610 pm. In the air they were ordered to patrol at 10,000 ft over a convoy off the East Anglian coast. Flying with them on this occasion was Martlesham's Station Commander, Wing Commander A. D. Farquhar, DFC, who had been one of the first fighter pilots to win the DFC in World War Two. He had commanded 602 (City of Glasgow) Squadron in the first months of the war and had accounted for three of the early German raiders over Scotland.

After patrolling over the ships for some ten minutes, Bayne looked to the south and saw anti-aircraft shells bursting. Through the November haze 17 Squadron soon spotted waves of Junker Ju87's, the well-known Stuka dive-bombers, fast approaching. Bayne immediately ordered his pilots into the attack, quickly counting between 25 and 30 of the gull-shaped-winged Stukas. They were from III/StG1, led by Kapitan Helmut Mahlke, and were escorted by two fighter Jagdgeschwaders. For the pilots of 17 Squadron, frustrated for some weeks through little real action, it was indeed a field-day with targets a-plenty. They made a total of 26 combat claims after the battle, which resulted in 13 Stukas being claimed destroyed, six more 'probably destroyed' plus others damaged. Strangely enough, little attempt was made by the 109's above to come down and assist the Stukas, only two being actually seen to attempt to interfere with the Hurricanes.

Although records now indicate that the claims were over-optimistic, Alfred Bayne received the DFC for leading the attack, in which he personally claimed one Stuka and assisted in probably destroying two others. Squadron Leader Miller received a message the next day from Air Chief Marshal Dowding, C in C Fighter Command, congratulating the squadron on its magnificent victory.

One can only surmise what a fighter like Manfred Czernin would have done in this action if he had not been on leave. He was, after all, the squadron's most successful pilot in terms of air victories and as one brother pilot put it: 'If they [enemy aircraft] were about, he usually managed to do something about it.'

Manfred missed yet another big fight on November 11, when the Stukas of III/StG1 were again encountered, this time off Burnham-on-Crouch. The squadron led by Squadron Leader Miller claimed three for certain, and probably accounted for four more as well as claiming two Me109's plus another possible. This time the 109 escort did fight and Pilot Officer D. H. Wissler did not return. Sergeant R. D. Hogg was also killed when he crashed while landing at Manston.

Manfred returned from leave the following day when there was not only much talk of these two recent actions but also of the news of the appearance of the Italian Air Force, also on the 11th. Their friends in 257 Squadron, led by ex-17 Squadron member Flight Lieutenant Pete 'Cowboy' Blatchford, shot down several Fiat BR20's and escorting Fiat CR42's. In fact for the next few days everyone seemed to be seeing Italian aeroplanes in the area when in reality they did not show themselves. This happened to Manfred himself during a most interesting combat.

Manfred was convinced that his first and only contact with the Italian Air Force came on November 17, when for some strange and unknown reason his expert eyes mis-identified a formation of twin-engined Me110's for Italian BR20's.

On the 17th things began to happen soon after breakfast when, at 8048, 257 Squadron took-off from Martlesham followed at 0905 by 11 Hurricanes of 17 Squadron to form a convoy patrol. Soon after they became airborne, 17 were vectored onto course 310 to intercept an enemy raid of 50^{+} bandits. The enemy aircraft were sighted at 10,000 ft near RAF Wattisham and immediately turned east, diving fast. The Hurricanes, flying on a north-westerly course turned to port to intercept and joined combat at 0915 over Ipswich.

On this rather cloudy day, Manfred flying as Yellow One, became separated from the others in the turn and was suddenly alone.

The German formation comprised two groups of bomb-carrying Me110's of Erprobungs-Gruppe 210 (EG210) escorted by the 'Yellow-nosed' Me109's of Jagdgeschwader 26 (JG26), commanded and led that day by the German ace Oberstleutnant Adolf Galland, who at this time had over 50 air combat victories to his credit. Galland was a veteran of the Spanish Civil War and also the German invasion of Poland. He scored his first kills flying with JG27 during the Blitzkrieg, downing three RAF Hurricanes on May 12, 1940 over Belgium. Following the fall of France he was given command of the 3rd Gruppe of JG26 *'Schlageter'*, being promoted to Major on July 18. By September 1940 his total victories had reached 40 and he had received the Knights Cross to his Iron Cross and also the Oak Leaves. On November 1, 1940 he was put in complete command of JG26, promoted to Lieutenant Colonel, being acknowledged as one of the leading aces of the Luftwaffe fighter arm.

JG26's mission on November 17 was to fly as direct escort to EG210's Messerschmitts who in turn were to attack the RAF airfield at Wattisham. Briefed to fly to Ipswich, they were then to follow the railway line to Stowmarket. EG210 took off from Denain at 0815 hours (German time) each machine carrying two 500 kg bombs. Clouds, however, were found to cover the target and therefore the formation turned back towards their secondary target – Harwich.

17 Squadron now came on the scene and saw the Germans making their turn to the east, but Manfred having become separated from the others in the cloud, came out to find the leading group of Me110's, escorted by at least six 109's. The other Hurricanes only saw and came into contact with the second formation of 110's flying some distance behind the first group. Galland and his fighters

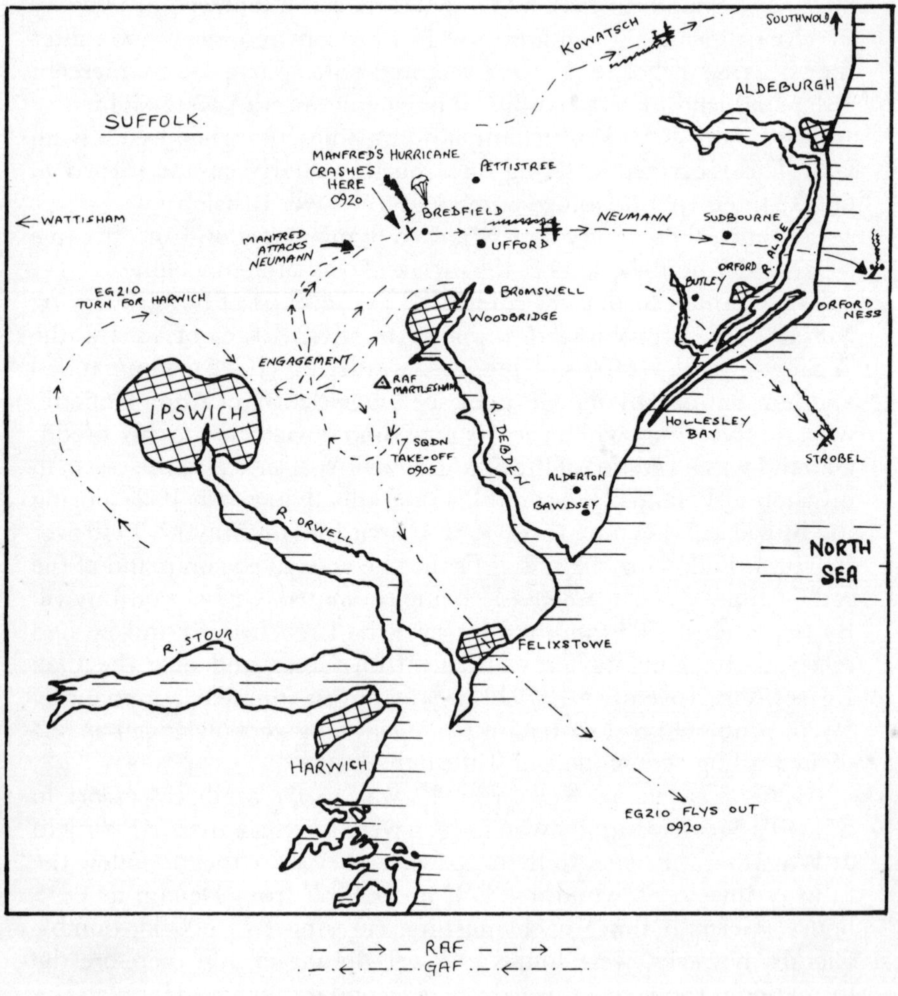

Sunday November 17, 1940

managed to prevent a total attack by the Hurricanes on the second formation, with constant sharp manoeuvres behind the 110's.

Manfred curved in behind the leading group and for some reason identified them as Italian Fiat BR20's. This to him was confirmed by what he recognised as Italian markings on the enemy aeroplanes. In that split second he undoubtedly hesitated when he was suddenly confronted by what he thought were men from the country he knew so well. In air combats moments of hesitation can be serious and allow the Grim Reaper to stretch out a hand. Manfred jabbed the gun button, seeing his fire hit the enemy and part of the tail fell away and one engine stopped and began to leave a trail of grey smoke. Galland flying above, spotted the Hurricane and saw it open fire on one of the rear Me110's, then he was diving down to attack. For a moment he lost sight of the British fighter because of the sun, then the Hurricane was in front of him. Galland's report stated:

> I immediately attacked this Hurricane from behind but I lost it for a moment because of the sun. I found it again after having left the formation sideways, and had the possibility to attack then from a distance of 150 – 50 metres from behind and sloping position. The Hurricane burst into flames and numerous metal parts (shot away) due to the well-concentrated fire. It went down steeply over the right wing with greyish-black smoke.

As Galland pulled up he looked down to see the 110 that Manfred had been attacking go down, leaving white smoke trails from both of its engines.

On the ground, Ron Buxton was getting in the horses for grooming on his father's farm, Red House Farm at Ufford. Hearing engines above he looked up and saw what he identified as a Dornier 17 with a Hurricane in pursuit. The noise sent the frightened animals galloping across the meadow and upon hearing machine gun fire, Ron threw himself down in the farmyard as the two aeroplanes passed over, heading south east towards Bromswell and the coast. Looking skywards again, he saw the Hurricane apparently hanging in the air at about cloud height with a slight bank to starboard. Cloud obscured his vision at that precise moment and he did not see Manfred leave the Hurricane.

The next thing to happen was the sound of the Merlin engine

increasing in intensity and then ceasing abruptly in a ground-jarring thud as the fighter disappeared from view and hit the ground. Both Ron and his brother observed the pilot floating gently earthwards and they set off in the direction it was travelling. They saw Manfred would land near the small village of Pettistree and began to proceed across country to where they estimated he would land. Arriving at a meadow, approximately one mile from the farm and next to Binghall Lane, Ufford, they saw Manfred hobbling across the field in their direction just as the police arrived, together with members of the Home Guard in a 15 cwt Bedford truck.

As soon as Galland's fire hit his Hurricane, Manfred knew his machine was finished. Almost at once his machine caught fire and the controls went limp. In that moment too he realised he was more frightened than he had ever been before. The Hurricane turned and began to roll over to the right and then the nose dropped; it was time to get out, and quick. Manfred unfastened his straps and slid back the cockpit canopy. Pulling off his flying helmet he heaved himself up and kicking himself free of the smoke-filled cockpit he leapt into space. His gloved fingers clutched at the metal 'D' ring, pulled it, and a second or two later he heard the satisfying crack above his head as the parachute opened and his fall was arrested with a jerk. He said a silent prayer to his maker and to the parachute packers, and strangely his thoughts returned to his early flying days and all those silly jokes about parachutes.

The roar of aero engines in his suddenly silent world brought him back to reality and looking over his shoulder he saw two Messerschmitt 109's coming towards him. Fearing that they might fire at him he tried to play dead, hanging his head and arms loosely. He was in fact fired on, but it is difficult to understand if it was two of Galland's pilots for the German made it clear to his men that on no account should they attempt to fire at any pilot in a parachute, although in the heat of combat anything can happen.

Flying nearby, and in full view of the whole affair was Sergeant Neil Cameron and he remembers seeing Manfred go down. 'I saw him bale out and descend by parachute and I know two Messerschmitt 109's shot at him during his descent and he tried to give the impression that he was dead.'

Meantime, his Hurricane, now well alight had gone down. As well as Ron Buxton and his brother, there were others who saw the happenings of that Sunday morning. Hearing the shooting and the roar of engines two farm workers out for a morning rabbit shoot, stood transfixed, gazing at the battle above them. This fascination did not last long because the descending Hurricane was coming their way looming ever larger. Yelling with fright they took to their heels for the nearest available ditch which was, unfortunately, very deep and very full, with obvious consequences as they dived in head first. The Hurricane crashed through a hedge losing both its wings then buried itself in the ground just west of, and within sight of, Bredfield Church – only a few feet from where the two rabbit hunters had been standing.

Ron Buxton left his brother to go across to the crash site arriving at the scene soon after the arrival of some RAF personnel who were discussing the wreck. The Hurricane (V7500) had entered the ground like a dart and left only the tail protruding, and Ron noticed that one of the wings had broken into smaller pieces on the opposite side of the hedge without damaging it. He stooped down and picked up one piece absolutely riddled with bullet holes. Underground the machine was still burning and he could hear the pop and crackle of exploding ammunition. The RAF later decided to remove enough of the Hurricane to clear plough depth and forget the rest.

Twenty nine years later, almost to the day, the remains of the Hurricane were excavated by Ian McLachlan with the help of his friend Ron Buxton and Mr Taylor on whose farm the Hurricane had crashed. Mr Taylor's memory of the event and of the exact location of the wreck was excellent and he pin-pointed the very spot, to within 24 inches, after 29 years and long after the nearby hedge had been removed.

In November 1969, with the help of a farm tractor, the Merlin engine, number 30527, together with the burnt and shattered remains of the cockpit, finally saw the light of day once again. Another item which had survived the years was the top section of the control column clearly showing the gun button that Manfred had pressed as he attacked the 110, or BR20 as he had thought.

Manfred came to earth and he too crashed through a hedge injuring his ankle. Stripping off his parachute he began to hobble across the fields towards the two Buxton boys but was then taken away by the Home Guard and the police. When he gave his name they took him to be a Polish pilot, recording this on their report. Shortly afterwards he was collected by a car from Martlesham and driven back to the airfield.

The other pilots of 17 Squadron had by this time, engaged the second formation of 110's; Alfred Bayne flying as Blue 1 (V7542) and Flying Officer Niemiec as his number two (V6759) attacked the rear section of 110's. Bayne closed behind two of them giving one short burst, observing his tracer going into its fuselage before he lost it in cloud. He then saw another and fired at it from 300 yards, then fired the rest of his ammunition into it. Both of the German's engines began to smoke but he was then attacked by three 110's and broke away.

Niemiec attacked No. 3 of the rear 110's firing a two second burst from 300 yards but without result. He then broke away as he was in turn engaged then saw two Me109's diving on Bayne and himself. Both 109's fired but from long range. Niemiec fired at one of these as it passed but saw no result.

Meanwhile Pilot Officer F. Kordula, Green 2, (P3023) and Sergeant Cameron as Green three (V7007), attacked 110's, Kordula attacking the leading vic and firing a three second burst. The section broke outwards and Kordula got in another burst on No 1 of the group but again saw no results from his fire. Passing through clouds he saw a 110 and chased it north east firing four short bursts. The German machine crossed the coast near Southwold and he last saw it out to sea at 2,000 ft with its starboard engine smoking badly.

Cameron attacked three 110's seeing one with its port engine on fire. He chased them across the coast near Aldeburgh but did not see any of them crash.

Chelmecki attacked and drove off one Me109 which was attempting to strafe shipping but it got away.

One 110 crashed into the sea at Aldeburgh and two more were reported by searchlight post FF35 at Butley, to have crossed the coast at less than 2,000 ft on fire and losing height. As it was impossible to state with any certainty which attacks were responsible the following credits were given:

Flight Lieutenant Bayne	1 Me110 destroyed, 1 Me110 damaged
Pilot Officer Kordula	$\frac{1}{2}$ Me110 destroyed, 1 Me110 damaged
Flying Officer Niemiec	$\frac{1}{2}$ Me110 destroyed

Sergeant Cameron	1 Me110 destroyed
Flying Officer Czernin	1 BR20 damaged.

Erprobungs-Gruppe 210 lost three of their aircraft that Sunday; Unteroffizier Hermann Strobel and his rear gunner were the crew of the 110 which went into the sea off Dunkirk, both men being killed. Unteroffizier Johann Kowatsch and his crewman were reported missing, while Unteroffizier Werner Neumann and his wireless operator, Obergefreite Karl Stoff became prisoners of war. Neumann of I/EG210 was hit badly during combat and both engines were damaged. He broke formation and made an attempt to reach the coast, being seen from the ground to fly low over Sudbourne leaving a trail of smoke.

Realising he would not be able to get across the sea he ordered Stoff to bale out, which he did, while Neumann left a few moments later. Stoff landed safely on land, Neumann splashing down into the sea.

Being rescued, he was most upset at being shot down and taken prisoner, his rescuers, the crew of the Aldeburgh lifeboat, thinking him a typical, arrogant Nazi, just like the popular press informed them all Germans were. Stoff was rather shaken by his ordeal and was reputedly afraid of what was going to happen to him. Neumann was apparently made of sterner stuff, hiding any. apprehension by his arrogant attitude.

The other 110's flew across the coast at Harwich and Felixstowe, nine were observed approaching from the north-east at 0920 am. They dropped at least eight of their 500 kg bombs on Languard Common near the Sewar Outfall Works, the Dock, and on RAF Station Felixstowe. One private of the 5th Battalion of the Manchester Regiment was killed, while another private and three civilians were injured, one of the latter dying later. Some damage was inflicted to the sewer and some RAF buildings also sustained some damage.

Adolf Galland together with six of his pilots flew over the coast and were engaged by the Hurricanes of 257 Squadron, who had seen nothing of the Me110 formation. The two groups clashed ten miles east of Harwich and in the ensuing dog-fight, 257 claimed to have shot down two of the 109s and probably another. Galland made his second kill of the mission when he sent Sergeant B. Henson, an experienced NCO pilot with at least two victories, into the sea east of the Lightship Sunk. Pilot Officer Mortimer was also hit, being wounded in the left hand by an exploding cannon shell, but he returned to land safely.

Galland had been flying a Messerschmitt bf 109 E-4 on this mission and his report shows that he had fired 67 rounds of 20 mm ammunition and 260 rounds on 7.8 mm ammunition.

Adolf Galland continued to command JG26 into 1941, until his friend Werner Molders was killed in a flying accident. Almost immediately, Hermann Goering, head of the German Luftwaffe, promoted Galland to General of the Fighter Arm. He ended the war with 104 combat victories, having received the highest German awards for bravery.

Manfred's victims, Neumann and Stoff, had both joined the Luftwaffe in November 1938, being teamed up together during their training at the Zerstoerer School at Schleissheim in April 1940. As a crew they were posted to 1 Staffel of EG210 on July 7, 1940, while this special unit was forming at Koln-Ostheim. With Me110 aeroplanes, mostly supplied by 1/ZG1, EG210 moved to Denain on July 10. By November 17, Neumann and Stoff had carried out 14 missions over England and both had been awarded the Iron Cross 2nd Class. The November 17 sortie was their first, following fourteen days leave which had commenced on October 16.

The combat between the Messerschmitts of Erprobungs-Gruppe 210 and the Hurricanes of 17 Squadron is as interesting as it is confused. If one studies the action in detail one is struck by the fact that none of the Royal Air Force pilots actually saw any of their opponents go down and crash; their subsequent claims written into their combat reports were confirmed later by the number of German machines known or rather believed to have been brought down. Surprisingly, the German lost the same number as the RAF pilots claimed, ie: three.

From all the available evidence it would seem that Alfred Bayne had crippled the Me110 flown by Hermann Strobel (an Me110 E-2 Werk No 3465, coded S9+LK); certainly Bayne mentioned the village of Butley in his Combat Report and it was the searchlight post at Butley that reported seeing a 110 cross the coast on fire and losing height. Strobel managed to nurse his aeroplane back across the North Sea but finally had to ditch just off the French Coast near Dunkirk. Both he and his gunner Obergefreite Willi Robermacher perished, their bodies being washed up some time later.

Pilot Officer Kordula, by the same token must have brought down Kowatsch, whose 110 (an Me110 C-4 Werk No 3648, coded S9+JK) the Czech pilot last saw on fire and losing height after it had crossed the coast at Southwold which was some 15 miles north of Butley. Johann Kowatsch and Unteroffizier Hans-Georg Bade were reported missing and presumably went into the North Sea somewhere. Bade's body was later washed up, but Kowatsch was never found.

The other point to be remembered is that, as far as can be ascertained, it was only the second formation of 110's that 17 attacked; this was 2/EG210 which lost two machines, Kowatsch and Strobel. 1/EG210 had been the lead group of 110's that Manfred had attacked. This group lost Neumann, and was the 110 that Galland reported to have gone down after Manfred's attack and did not get back to France. There is every reason, therefore, to believe that Manfred's fire did the damage and Neumann only managed to get his crippled fighter as far as the English coast. Whether it was in fact attacked again while in this damaged state (it certainly appeared to have flown through the area of the main fight) may never be known. Manfred of course had only claimed an Italian BR20 as damaged, so would not have had any reason to think that any of the 110's were his, but it certainly looks as if his fire did the damage.

Again one can only wonder why a man like Manfred with his vast experience, identified the 110 as a BR20 in the first place; after all he had fought enough of the former, and indeed he had already shot down seven of the type. To add to the dilemma, Eric Lock, another very experienced pilot flying with 41 Squadron, also reported sighting Italian aeroplanes that morning in the same area. Lock, during a combat, shot down two 109's before being badly wounded himself, coming down in a force-landing at Buckenay Farm, Alderton. Why these men should claim to see Italians that day is odd, and certainly the Italian Air Force claim not to have flown any sorties on the 17th. Could it be perhaps that EG210, this special, almost élite group, were carrying Italian markings that day to confuse the British defences or to boost their Axis comrade's propaganda? Perhaps we shall never know the answer.

Manfred was pensive after being shot down and was shaken because he had found himself praying while dropping through the air prior to his parachute opening. He had thought himself an unbeliever.

He flew again on the 19th following his entry into the 'Caterpillar Club', the club exclusive to those men who had been saved by parachute descent, when with other members of the squadron he did a 'beat-up' of the aerodrome on the occasion of Squadron Leader Tony Miller's wedding, which took place at Woodbridge. Later that day he was ordered up after an unidentified aircraft which he engaged, but it was too fast for him and he lost it in the clouds.

This ended the air action for him and his brother pilots during that fateful summer of 1940, although patrols and scrambles continued for the remaining weeks of that year. The official date for the ending of the Battle of Britain was October 31 and 17 Squadron had made its contribution to the Royal Air Force's most important and gallant victory.

Before leaving this chapter of Manfred's part in the air war over France and England, perhaps some assessment and comment on his capabilities from the men who flew with him in action might be appropriate.

Harold Bird-Wilson, who as already mentioned was shot down and wounded by an Me109 in September 1940 but who later returned to operations and completed over 600 operational sorties with the RAF, remembers Manfred most vividly:

'Manfred's flying ability was well above the average and he quickly settled down in A Flight, 17 Squadron, and became a section leader. It was during the Battle of Britain that he impressed me with his answer to the defensive circle that the Me110's were adopting. To most pilots it was extremely hard to penetrate this German tactic once the Me's had formed up. It was Manfred's firm conviction that the only way to attack the Me110's was to carry out a head-on attack and go round in a circle in the opposite direction to the Germans'. This may have not been a very successful manoeuvre to shoot down Me110's but it usually meant that the formation broke up and thus became easier kills for fellow RAF pilots. Additionally, he always carried out his attacks against German aircraft with sheer determination and courage. He was the bravest man I ever knew.'

Neil Cameron who later flew in Russia, North Africa and Burma relates:

'I was in 17 Squadron with Czernin during the latter part of the Battle of Britain and subsequently. He was deputy Flight Commander in A Flight, whilst I was in B Flight. I am sure there is no need to tell you that he was an extremely colourful character and though, in my estimation, his actual flying ability was not of the highest standard, he was undoubtedly one of the best shots in the business.'

Leonard Bartlett who was with Manfred during the fight over Portland on August 25, and often flew in Manfred's section, also remembers him:

'He was a fearless chap, a fantastically good shot, but not an outstanding tactician or pilot. He was very shaken when he spun out of cloud when his artificial horizon toppled. He didn't know that this happened if the aircraft was manoeuvred beyond 45 degree angle when the AF was uncaged. It would not be true to say that he was popular with his brother pilots, mainly because he was flamboyant and tended to shoot a line but he was a fearless man and an above the average fighter pilot.'

Glyn Griffiths also remembers the episode when Manfred spun out of the clouds. He landed very shaken and as white as a sheet. His lips had lost their colour and he was sick. In lighter vein, Griffiths recalls that Manfred often wore a camel hair coat and red scarf over his RAF uniform. Quite against King's Regulations but it seemed to be accepted within reason. Griffiths did valuable work with 17 Squadron and received the DFM on November 12, 1940.

Desmond Fopp has his recollections too:

'My personal view of the Count was that he was a typical fighter-pilot of the time. He enjoyed parties and flying and was good at both. He was to my mind like most Czechs (sic) an individualist in the air rather than a leader, but as these were relatively early days he may well have developed these qualities at a later date.'

CHAPTER SEVEN

Instructor and Squadron Commander

Flying Officer Count Manfred Czernin, holder of the Distinguished Flying Cross, had made a personal contribution to the Battle of Britain that was not inconsiderable. Because of his Czech-Austrian backgrund, his exploits were little known outside his immediate RAF circle, although he had gained some amusing publicity as already related in the previous chapter. In any event his score of enemy aeroplanes brought down as a fighter pilot was not mentioned in the so-called ace lists popular at the time.

His material gains throughout 1940 were above the average in terms of enemy aircraft shot down or damaged. During the year he had personally been credited with the following successes:

Enemy aircraft personally destroyed	13
Enemy aircraft shared destroyed	6
Aircraft destroyed but unconfirmed	2
Enemy aircraft 'probably' destroyed	2
Enemy aircraft 'damaged'	5
Enemy aircraft shared 'damaged'	2

This represents a total of 30 German aircraft destroyed or damaged in air combat. Of his 19 confirmed successes, ten had been twin-engined bombers, seven had been twin-engined fighters or fighter-bombers, one a single-engined fighter and one an Army Co-operation machine. During the actual Battle period, July 1 to October 31, he had destroyed eight and shared in the destruction of six more. For those interested in fractions his score during this period could be said to be 10 confirmed victories or overall a total of 15.

For the year of 1940 he was in fact one of the top twenty RAF fighter pilots as regards victories, and if his successes are compared with the more well-known of his contemporaries, he matches up quite well. 'Sailor' Malan, the South African pilot who flew with 74 Squadron, had around 18 victories by the end of 1940, while Al Deere from New Zealand flying with 54 Squadron gained 17 and Douglas Bader of 242 Squadron had 12½.

During the actual Battle, Manfred had flown a total of 125 operational flying hours, involving 72 scrambles, 15 convoy and 10 routine patrols, making a total of 97 operational sorties.

December 28 was a sad day for 17 Squadron, for Pilot Officer David Leary, DFC, a pilot who had fought valiantly during the summer was killed when he attacked a Dornier and was hit by return fire. Leary had served in France earlier and had been credited with at least six victories. Three days later the fateful year of 1940 came to an end.

For the Royal Air Force, and for Fighter Command, 1941 was, for all everybody really knew, going to be another long struggle with the German Air Force. While they waited for the spring and the renewed activity that in fact, as far as daylight raids were concerned, never came, the squadron still prepared itself for action. Convoy patrols were still flown during the cold wintry days of January with the occasional scramble thrown in. On February 2, Manfred leading Yellow section with Kumiega and Bartlett, took-off at 1525 hours to intercept a lone twin-engined Junkers 88 that had been reported east of Lowestoft at 5,000 ft. The enemy bomber was sighted but as the Hurricanes closed in the Junkers slipped into cloud cover and they lost it. Manfred landed back at base and taxied to the dispersal area. As he undid his straps and heaved himself out of the cockpit his ground crew began inspecting his machine.

'He got you then, sir,' observed his mechanic.

'What's that?' asked Manfred.

'He got you, sir. Look here, two bullet holes.'

Manfred jumped to the ground and inspected the holes that he mechanic was indicating. Sure enough, the German rear gunner must have fired off a quick burst at him as they closed in, hitting the Hurricane in two places. One bullet had damaged the petrol tank while the other had hit the port mainplane.

During the latter half of February convoy patrols were flown with the occasional scramble but the only important event came on the 28th. The squadron began to receive their first Hawker Hurricane Mark II, Manfred having a test flight on the last day of the month. After landing following a forty minute test flight he entered the record in his log-book adding two words which apparently summed up his impression of the newer machine. The two words were 'Oh boy!'

An even more important but personal event occurred in February when he attended Buckingham Palace to meet his King and to receive his Distinguished Flying Cross. He was one of 52 officers receiving this decoration which was the same investiture at which Louis Mountbatten received the award of the DSO. As always there were several photographers outside the Palace, taking pictures of the heroes, and one or two appeared of Manfred in various newspapers and magazines. He had been accompanied by Maud and his mother but one picture which appeared showing the three of them walking away from the Palace gates was captioned: 'Flying Officer Czernin, seen here with his wife and daughter ...'

With the slightly improved weather in March, Manfred, who was promoted to Flight Lieutenant on the 19th, taking over the command of A Flight from Flight Lieutenant Harper four days later when Harper went to 57 OTU, flew 18 patrols over the south coast of England. All proved uneventful until a convoy patrol on the 25th.

Flight Lieutenant Alfred Bayne led blue section out over the convoy at 0940, to be relieved by Manfred's Red Section later that morning. Manfred took-off at 1025, Squadron Leader Henry Woodhouse, flying with the squadron to gain combat experience, flying as Manfred's Number Two. As they relieved Bayne, Manfred saw anti-aircraft shells bursting above the ships below and just had time to see several Me109s diving down at his patrol.

'Look-out Red Leader, 109s, break starboard!'

Manfred heard the warning in the same instant and without thinking, he automatically slammed the throttle forward, kicked the rudder and heaved the stick back and to the right. He felt rather than saw the leading Messerschmitt but he did see the lines of tracer shells which streaked over his perspex cockpit hood.

'Keep turning,' he thought to himself, 'keep turning.' He saw two more Messerschmitts diving down and could see two tiny flashing lights on the top of the leading aircraft's engine cowling, as the

Partisans parade through the streets of Bergamo, June 1945. Renato Fasana (saluting the camera) leads one group past the Police "Prefettura" in the Via Torquato Tassa and on towards the Piazza Vittorio Veneto and the Town Hall.

The smiles of victory! Capt Pearson, Manfred, Zaverio Fornoni, "Moicano" Poduje, Bepi Lanfranchi, Piero Redaelli, Joseph --, front row: Giuseppe Digorini, Noe Trezzi, Giuliano Mattioli, (Manfred's second-in-command) and Lino Chiapparini.

German pilot fired into the group of scattering Hurricanes.

Manfred saw one Messerschmitt on the tail of Squadron Leader Woodhouse who had not been able to keep with Manfred in the tight turn. Manfred turned quickly in behind the German but was unable to get in a burst before the enemy pilot, seeing the danger behind him, pulled up into cloud.

'Reform, reform.' Manfred thankfully counted all his machines, grateful and relieved that nobody had been hit.

Manfred took a few days leave at the beginning of April, spending a restful time with Maud who, carrying their first child, was nearing the time of the birth. Arrangements had already been made with the Crescent Nursing Home, Windsor, for the event and when Manfred left to rejoin 17 Squadron for what was to be his last few weeks with the unit, he was looking forward to receiving the call that would tell him he was a father.

Early in April, 17 Squadron moved north to Casteltown, where Manfred spent his last weeks with them, patrolling and being sent up after elusive day and night raiders. He was now due for a rest from operational flying, having been on active duty for 15 months.

Just before he left the squadron, his wife Maud presented him with a daughter on May 9, the child being named Carolyn. The birth took place at Windsor where Maud and Mrs Frost were staying for this special event. His mother telegraphed the news to Manfred who was immediately given 48 hours leave. He arrived in London the next evening, May 10, 1941, the night the Germans launched one of their greatest night raids of the Blitz. Making his way across the city, with bombs raining down, he passed St George's Hospital, which had just received a direct hit. Manfred stopped his journey and spent the rest of the night helping to fight the fires and assisting with the dead and injured. When he finally arrived at Windsor, his mother asked him how he could waste so much time when his wife and baby were waiting for him. Indeed, he might even have been killed or injured. His reply was one that she was often to hear from him later.

'Why worry?' he said with a smile. 'There is only one bullet forged for you and so long as it hasn't come, nothing will happen, and when it does, nothing will save you.'

Manfred left the squadron at the end of May, posted to Number

52 OTU (Operational Training Unit). He left as the unit's top-scoring fighter pilot and no other pilot was to beat his score in WW2. In 1941 most of the pilots who had been with 17 during the previous year began to disperse and go their separate ways and soon the old 17 was gone forever.

Harold Bird-Wilson, who had left the squadron suddenly on September 24, after being shot down by a 109, returned to operations in April 1941 as a flight commander in 234 Squadron. He ended the war as wing commander. Neil Cameron went to 134 Squadron in 1941 and with them went to Russia in the early summer. He was later to fly in North Africa and ended the war in command of a fighter squadron in Burma.

Desmond Fopp, who had been shot down on September 3, returned to 17 Squadron in 1941. He had, following his period in hospital, been posted to No 3 School of General Reconnaissance in January 1941, converting onto Avro Ansons and Blackburn Botha aircraft for a so-called rest! He purposefully made such a nuisance of himself that he was posted back to his old squadron, later returning to operations with 132 Squadron.

Glyn Griffiths became an instructor in 1941, going to Canada to carry out these important duties. Being commissioned, he later returned to England to fly operationally with 4 Squadron flying Mustangs in 1944. When returning from a mission over France on one occasion his Number Two collided with his Mustang over their base at RAF Odiham, and he was badly burned before he managed to bale out. By the time he recovered from his injuries the war had ended.

Leonard Bartlett left the squadron and later served in the Middle East, then took command of 253 Squadron, receiving the DSO. He eventually rose to the rank of Group Captain, and was one of the Battle of Britain pilot escort at Sir Winston Churchill's funeral. Alfred Bayne went to 132 Squadron in April 1941, going on to command 30 Squadron in Ceylon but sadly he did not survive the war.

Number 52 Operational Training Unit was at RAF Debden, commanded by Group Captain D. M. Fleming. Taking up his new post Manfred was put in charge of A Squadron.

He arrived on June 3, the Unit's Record Book noting his arrival and placing the nationality (British) after his name! This was not too surprising bearing in mind the many nationalities that passed through Training Command in 1941. There were French, Norwegian, Polish and Czech as well as men from the Commonwealth and the Dominions.

There were several well-known and highly successful pilots at 52 OTU in the early summer of 1941, all passing their experience onto the new generation of fighter pilots. In July, for instance, the Officer Commanding the Training Wing was Squadron Leader John Grandy who had commanded 249 Squadron in 1940. The Chief Flying Instructor was Squadron Leader C. F. 'Bunny' Currant, DFC and bar, an experienced pilot, having gained 14 victories during the Battle of Britain, flying with 605 Squadron. Manfred had A Squadron; B Squadron was led by Flight Lieutenant Andy McDowell, DFM and bar, who had also shot down 14 enemy aircraft during 1940 with 602 Squadron, before being commissioned. An old friend from 85 Squadron, Flight Lieutenant A. G. Lewis, DFC and bar, led C Squadron, following a successful period with the old squadron and later with 249 Squadron. Gerald Lewis had 18 victories at this time. D Squadron was under the leadership of Flight Lieutenant P. G. H. Matthews, DFC, who had gained several victories with 1 Squadron in both France and during the Battle of Britain. E Squadron was led by Flight Lieutenant J. R. H. Lewis.

Other pilots who were instructors at the Unit were Flight Lieutenant Frank Carey, DFC and bar DFM, with 18 victories flying with 43 Squadron and who would go on to score nearly 30 (he left on July 25). and Flight Lieutenant Keith Lofts DFC, with 8 or 9 kills gained while serving with 615 and 249 Squadrons, again in both France and over England. He left on July 30.

Manfred still flew the Hawker Hurricane while instructing dual on the Miles Master, taking the student pilot through all the various exercises to bring them to an operational readiness. In July 52 OTU moved from Debden to Aston Down and when 'Bunny' Currant left to go to 501 Squadron on August 14, a new CFI, Flight Lieutenant F. M. Smith, DFC, was posted in from RAF Hornchurch, to fill this post.

Forgrave Smith, a Canadian, had joined the RAF in 1936 and was known to his friends as 'Hiram'. In 1940 he had been a flight commander with 72 Squadron, flying Spitfires, fighting during the Battle of Britain until he was shot down and badly wounded in August. Recovering from his wounds he commanded 603 Squadron in 1941 before becoming CFI at 52 OTU. He and Manfred became close friends, no doubt drawn together by the fact that they had both been pre-war pilots and also because they were both older than the average young pilots that passed through their hands at Aston Down. And they were many. In July for instance, the Unit flew 3,948 flying hours with some 90 pupils going through Training Courses 6 and 7. On strength the Unit had some 60 odd Hurricanes plus 25 training types.

Hiram Smith remembers meeting Manfred in 1941, and it was clear that even then some of Manfred's associates were still not clear just where the Count originated from:

'It was in August 1941 that I went to 52 OTU and met Czernin for the first time. Needless to say he was something of a novelty – a fighter-pilot Count in the RAF from (apparently) Central Europe, and there seemed some doubt as to whether his native land was Czechoslovakia, Austria or both. I would say that he was a very good pilot, who had considerable flair and dash. He was also very much an extrovert and was not unduly modest. These qualities enabled him to make a considerable impression on young trainee pilots. For instance he would read them his combat reports, a practice which was frowned on as 'line-shooting' by some of the other instructors, but I have no doubt it was stimulating and educational to the students.'

In spite of his marriage to Maud, it would be inaccurate not to mention that in making many friends Manfred was also a continued success with the ladies, who always played a prominent part in his social activities. The ladies not unnaturally found him a most attractive proposition. At 28 years of age he was a mature, tall, good looking man. Fair, though slightly thinning, hair did not detract in any way from his good looks. His general personality was pleasing and his way of introducing himself as a Count always impressed, and of course fighter-pilots with the DFC were all the rage. He was very much the hero, and liked it.

He had become a great gambler on the horses and at cards, being most skilful at poker which he played successfully and with some enthusiasm, fully expecting novices to the game to be indoctrinated the hard way.

At Aston Down in 1941 there were three Czechoslovakian pilots on the instructional staff, their names being Kausky, Cukr and Kopesky. It can be assumed that they were somewhat left of centre politically and they seemed to react rather suspiciously towards Manfred, the aristocratic Count. Their attitude may be likened to that shown towards an absentee landlord or in this particular case an ex-landlord. Probably their attitude changed later, especially when it is remembered that after the war both Cukr and Kausky escaped from their communist controlled country, the latter making a most spectacular getaway by flying over the Iron Curtain in an aeroplane. In any event all three had flown during the Battle of Britain as Sergeant pilots, and no doubt they had some feelings of admiration for Manfred's achievements.

On August 8, Flight Lieutenant Harold Bird-Wilson, DFC, arrived at 52 OTU from 234 Squadron as an instructor. This was a happy re-union for Manfred, being able, once again, to be with his old friend from 17 Squadron. When Manfred left the Unit on December 16, 'Birdy' took over A Squadron from Manfred.

Manfred completed his six months 'rest' period as an instructor, the only real flight out of the normal routine of tests, being on September 10, 1941. On that day aircraft from Aston Down flew low-level over Gloucester, Cheltenham and Stroud in a splendid beat-up in aid of War Weapons Week.

Promoted to Acting Squadron Leader he was given command of 65 Squadron who were based at his old haunt of Tangmere. 65 were equipped with the Spitfire Vb, Manfred having already tasted the delights of this famous aeroplane as Aston Down. He remained with 65 Squadron for only a week during which time he flew only one operational sortie, flown on December 19. Leading the squadron they flew on a routine shipping patrol but when the squadron was relieved Manfred could not resist curving south to do a quick beat-up of enemy held Calais, and getting shot at by flak as he streaked over the town and harbour.

Three days later he took command of 222 Squadron at North Weald where he spent his third wartime Christmas. He took over from Squadron Leader H. T. Gilbert, until recently a flight commander with 71 (Eagle) Squadron, who swopping with Manfred, went to lead 65 Squadron. Manfred flew one sortie with 222, leading twelve aircraft on a patrol over some minesweepers along the coast on December 28. On January 19, 1942, Squadron Leader R. M. Milne, DFC and bar, arrived to take command.

Manfred was on the move again, being attached to 41 Squadron based at West Hamptnett, Sussex, again flying the Spitfire. With them he flew several sorties and it felt good to be back on operations again. The unit also operated from Tangmere during January and February 1942 and in the main these sorties were shipping reconnaissance missions off the French coast or search and rescue patrols, looking for downed pilots and aircrew in the Channel. As always, he preferred to fly a machine with the code letter 'F' painted on the fuselage and with 41 Squadron he took over a machine marked 'E' which he then had altered to 'F'. It was undoubtedly one of those pilot superstitions that grew up. He had flown an 'F' successfully during the Battle of Britain, and so whenever he could he used a machine marked 'F' thereafter.

On February 12 the German warships *Scharnhorst* and *Gneisenau* made their famous Channel Dash up the English Channel from Brest. During the day 41 Squadron escorted bomb-carrying Hurricanes and Bristol Beaufort torpedo bombers in attacks on these ships. Squadron Leader P. 'Dutch' Hugo led the Spitfires, Manfred flying at the head of Green Section at 1230 pm. Some of the squadron encountered some Me109s, three being shot down and a fourth damaged. Two more missions were flown that day but without any contact with the enemy. They finally landed at Manston after encountering much heavy and not inaccurate anti-aircraft fire from the ships and their escorts. Manfred's last sortie from England took place on February 13, when he led a fighter sweep over the Channel between 1355 and 1510 hours.

Manfred now received orders to proceed overseas. He was 29 years old now, too old for a fighter-pilot but his vast experience and proven leadership was needed in yet another role, but this time he was required half-way around the world. Leaving England was a challenge although the personal upheaval was considerable. With Japan's entry into the war following their attack on Pearl Harbour in December 1941, British interests and bases in the Far East were in danger and Manfred was one of the many chosen to be sent to this new theatre of operations. In fact many pilots who had flown during the Battle of Britain as junior officers, like Manfred, were now put in command of units in the Far East. Men like Ginger Lacey, Frank Carey, Barry Sutton etc: At the end of February, therefore, he left England and went to India.

Initially he was attached to 301 Maintenance Unit until March 16. Then came a posting to India where he was given command of

146 Squadron again being able to fly the big, powerful Hawker Hurricane. One sad sidelight to this posting concerned his faithful elkhound Kyro. Until now Kyro had always been able to move from base to base with his master, always accepted by the other pilots and ground crews. He would wait patiently for Manfred to return from a flight or sortie. He had now to be left behind, and soon began to pine for Manfred, not understanding why he did not come for him. No one could feed or comfort the poor animal and within a short while he died.

Manfred arrived at his new command on March 31, 1942, taking over from Squadron Leader Bertram Barthold, who then became station CO. 146 Squadron was a composite unit based at Dinjan in Upper Assam and Manfred's first task on taking command was to properly organise and prepare his squadron, which, together with another composite unit, 5 Squadron, was the only fighter defence in that region. Together with his senior flight commander, Flight Lieutenant Ian L. B. Aitkens, they set-to with the task in hand.

At the beginning of April there was a relative calm following the hectic weeks of the Allied retreat before the Imperial Japanese forces during February and March. Aeroplanes and essential spares were still in short supply although these were soon to arrive in the coming weeks. During this interim period both squadrons flew Curtiss Mohawks and Hurricanes.

146 Squadron had an assortment of machines really, Hurricanes, Mohawks, Brewater Buffaloes and even old Hawker Audax – vintage 1931. The Audax, however, brought back pleasant memories to Manfred, who had not flown this old two-seater biplane since his early training days.

Manfred's first operational sorties came on April 5 when, as Hurricanes were still few on the ground, he flew a Mohawk. In the morning sortie he took off and flew a sector reconnaissance mission and later in the day there came an alert and he and his flight commander were scrambled but found nothing. He took off during another flap on the 7th and on the 10th flew an Audax on yet another reconnaissance mission.

Office and paper work took up more of his time but he found a spare few moments on the 20th to fly down to Dumdum in an Audax, taking Lieutenant Rowe with him, and a couple of days later he returned in a spare Mohawk. Manfred was now becoming more satisfied with his squadron and during early May intensive practice flights were carried out, including night flying.

On May 5, 224 Group Headquarters ordered redeployment of both units as follows:

5 Squadron. All pilots and 50 ground crew posted to Dinjan. 146 Squadron. All pilots, two Buffaloes and three Audax aircraft with 50 ground crew to Jessore, later amended to Dumdum.

Those personnel of 146 left at Dumdum reformed number 5 Squadron, while pilots of 5 Squadron left at Dumdum reformed 146 Squadron.

Manfred and the remainder of 146 left for Dumdum on May 8 to link up with the newly formed half. Manfred and Flight Lieutenant Aitkens flew in Buffaloes while Flight Lieutenant Coombs, Lieutenant Rowe and Sergeant Davidson flew in the three Audax with Pilot Officer Hartly and Sergeants Gill and Collins as passengers.

Manfred arrived safely but Aitkens crashed at Jessore, wrote off his aeroplane and put himself in hospital. Flying Officer Boyd and 50 ground crew personnel travelled by rail, arriving on the 11th. 146 was now re-equipped totally with Hurricanes between May 15 and 25th and intensive training was put into effect at Dumdum, where they shared the airfield with 135 Squadron, these two units comprising the Wing.

On June 15, both units were able to implement squadron readiness states; up until now only Flight readiness was possible in conjunction with 135.

From June 20 to 26 night flying training was put into force, but then on the 29th the Monsoon broke. Training continued when possible and exercises flown. On August 8 the squadron was scrambled at 0520 but no enemy aircraft were found. The unit remained at readiness for the rest of the day but without incident. As a precaution against rioters and saboteurs, night guards were posted around the airfield and the guard on the aeroplanes doubled.

The squadron was ordered to Alipone on August 21 but then the move was postponed for one week. The next day 146 were scrambled again at 1500 but still no enemy machines appeared.

Railway patrols were ordered at this time, flown by sections of two Hurricanes along the rail track between Cuttack and Berhampore in case saboteurs attempted to cut the track.

Flight Lieutenant Aitkens, recently returned from hospital, was posted to 17 Squadron on August 26, and that same day nine aircraft were scrambled at 0820 when six Japanese aircraft were reported approaching but they must have turned back for they were not seen.

The move to Alipore finally came on September 6, and Manfred and his two flight commanders, Flight Lieutenants M. W. Coombes and H. P. D. Sykes sorted out all the problems. On the 14th a Japanese recce: aeroplane was reported but again the machines sent up found nothing. Manfred then left for two weeks leave and command of 146 went to Squadron Leader Peter M. Bond. Manfred returned to 146 on October 5 in time for a visit by the Governor of India and Air Vice Marshal D. F. Stevenson.

During October and November Manfred flew several offensive patrols over the jungle and took-off on several alerts but no enemy machines were ever encountered. During October, happy news was received from home, for on the 12th of that month Manfred's son Nicholas was born. He was to grow tall, slim and good looking like his father, whom he was to resemble very much.

Manfred was now feeling the total effects of almost three years of flying, both on operations and as an instructor, finally having the exacting task of squadron commander in jungle airstrips which taxed his reserves of strength and energy. On November 27 he was posted to 224 Group Head-Quarters as a Staff Officer in Operations, command of 146 Squadron passing to Squadron Leader Geoffrey Williams.

When he arrived for duties with 224 Group he was nearing a total collapse. On January 15, 1943 he was sent up into the mountains to a medical centre, for both rest and medical attention. Returning to duty on February 2 he was again on the sick list between March 25 and April 3. Finally his posting to the United Kingdom came through and he was sent to British HQ, Bombay, pending embarkation for England in mid-April. During his period with 224 Group he flew only twice. Once on November 27 when he flew to his new post in a Hurricane, and then in February 1943 when he took another Hurricane on a flight from Rajyeswarpur to Chittagong between the 21st and 23rd. The next time he flew to war it was to be as a passenger.

One little note of interest while he was with the 224 Group was an entry in the Group's records, that Acting Squadron Leader Lord W. Waleron with the A & SD (Intelligence) arrived to carry out certain duties between January and April 1943. No doubt Manfred and his best man at his wedding, spent many happy evenings chatting over old times.

Once back in the UK he hoped to be given the command of another squadron and even return to operations but his requests were evaded. Now at the age of 30 he was obviously too old for high speed fighter combat where split-second reflexes were essential. Death for himself and possibly for those under his leadership could result if the quickness of youth, no longer his, delayed a manoeuvre or a decision. So he spent long dreary weeks at RAF Uxbridge, feeling no doubt and looking very miserable. He was, however, able to see his two children being stationed so near London and naturally he was able to enjoy once again the pleasures of the city he loved and often dreamt of while in India.

Whenever he could, he would go to the Air Ministry and try to get some answers from the powers that be and during one of these visits Manfred was spotted by an Air Marshal as he sat dejectedly in a corridor. The Air Marshal remembered the tall, good looking pilot from earlier, happier days.

'Hullo, Czernin, what are you doing now? You look rather bedraggled.' Manfred was pleased to see one of his former superiors and even more heartened that he should remember him.

'I'm a bit fed up, sir, I haven't got a job,' replied Manfred. The Air Marshal paused, looking deep into the Squadron Leader's eyes, seeing perhaps the years of struggle, the loyalty or strength of purpose written on Manfred's face. He turned slowly then looked again at Manfred.

'Come to my office tomorrow and we'll have a talk,' said the Air Marshal smiling, then walked away.

The following day Manfred returned to the Air Ministry early making his presence known to the Air Marshal's PA. After a short wait he was ushered in to see the man who might prove his benefactor. One can only guess at what words were spoken between the long serving Air Officer and the ex-fighter pilot but the result, for Manfred, was a new sense of purpose, another great challenge and a chance again to be the adventurer.

CHAPTER EIGHT

Special Operations
The First Mission

During the Second World War, there were few men who were able to show their mettle in two entirely different fields of action. Manfred Czernin, however, was one of those men who did have the opportunity and he proved as successful in the second as he had been in the first.

The direct result of his informal chat with the Air Marshal was that Manfred was given the opportunity for the action he craved for but of a very different nature from that of a Royal Air Force fighter pilot. It was, nevertheless, just the sort of job at which a man like Manfred would excel, once the idea and proposition had been put to him.

And so it was that in September 1943 the Royal Air Force noted its records and struck off Squadron Leader M. B. Czernin, DFC, from its list of operational officers and showed that he had been transferred to Air Ministry Unit, London, with effect from September 30. He had in fact been secretly posted to the ranks of the Special Operations Executive – the famed SOE. In this he must be unique, from being a successful fighter 'ace' to that of a Special Force Officer.

It can be said that the title Special Operations Executive – Winston Churchill's created force who were, to quote this great man's words, 'To set Europe ablaze' – covered a multitude of sins, but however literally this expression is taken it was a very special and efficient section of Britain's war effort. Sabotage, resistance work, demolition, cloak and dagger, partisans, espionage, are all words or phrases that could add up to the war waged by SOE behind the enemy's lines. To many people this work is associated with the nearer continental countries of France, Holland, Belgium and Norway etc; but Special Force would soon be operating in another country, a country which to a great extent was hostile to the Allies – Italy.

It is not difficult to see how well Manfred might fit into this sphere of operations at this particular stage of the war. He spoke fluent Italian, and it will be remembered that in 1937 he became an interpreter Second Class, in this language, could converse easily in French and had a knowledge of German. This, together with his Italian background with its intimate appreciation of the people, a love and detailed knowledge of the country, makes it easy to imagine just how much of an asset his superiors thought he might be in the Executive's new areas of operations in central and northern Italy.

The organisation formed within the overall framework of SOE to commence operations on the Italian mainland was called 'Number 1 Special Force. Its first Commanding Officer was a naval man, Commander Gerald (Gerry) Holdsworth, DSO OBE RNVR, and it was incorporated within the British 15th Army Group. Following the successful invasion of Italy itself, it was now time for the newly-formed unit of No. 1 Special Force to try and establish itself in this theatre of operations.

It was of course known and appreciated that not all Italian people were hostile towards the Allies. Many thousands of Italians hated, despised and totally opposed the dictatorial reign of Mussolini and his Fascist followers. Certainly now, when the fortunes of war were beginning to turn and engulf their own homeland, many more saw the hopelessness and futility of the Duce's plans and dreams. Being, to all intents and purposes, a hostile country, the members of No 1 Special Force would have to rely to a great degree on finding and cultivating these friendly elements if they were to succeed in their work, and initially this was probably the hardest part in the setting up of their organisation.

No 1 Special Force initially comprised of only five officers, including Commander Holdsworth, and his second in command Major Richard T. Hewitt. Under Holdsworth this group moved across to the heel of Italy where a base was set up at a place called

Monopoli on the Adriatic Coast. They then took over the Castle at Stefano which soon became the training school of the Force and the Group began to receive or have posted-in, officers and men as the unit became more established. 'Dick' Hewitt was later promoted to Lieutenant Colonel and took over command of the Force, a position he maintained until the end of the war. For his leadership and ability he received the OBE.

The Force, by the war's end, had a total of 160 officers and some 2,000 men, but this figure did not include men recruited in the field. Usually these recruits came in the form of escaped British prisoners of war, or those other prisoners released when Italy surrendered and who then chose to join with partisan groups. One of these was Major Gorden Lett DSO, whose memory greatly assisted the author in dealing with this part of Manfred's history, although he himself did not know him.

The base at Stefano was set up in September 1943 at about the same time as the Allies launched Operation 'Avalanche' known afterwards as the Salerno landing. Following this, on September 8, Italy surrendered. Not long after this armistice, officers and men of the Italian Army based in the German occupied parts of Northern Italy, particularly in the Piedmont and Alpine Valley regions, together with patriots from both the towns and the countryside, began to form themselves into Partisan bands. Their object was to operate against the Germans and the Fascists who continued to follow the dictates of Mussolini.

In the south, Marshal Badoglio formed and set in motion monarchist government at Brindisi in support of the King of Italy, which was in part recognised by the Allied powers. It was not long before the northern Partisans began to make contact with British and American Armies south of Rome and with the Badoglio government, asking for help, support and supplies. Number 1 Special Force was suddenly in business.

In the next few months the organisation of Italian resistance was set in motion. However, these initial Partisan formations did not immediately present a military threat to the Germans or to the Fascist forces and it took some time for them to develop into an operational command. The Germans had by this time not retreated to the more northerly regions of Italy as had first been hoped but had swiftly sent troops into the unoccupied mid-regions and marched into the capital, Rome. It became obvious that they were fully prepared to fight for every yard of the Italian mainland that remained.

As the Partisans began to form, patriotic workers in the industrial towns and centres began delaying actions in the factories, one particular method being strike action which delayed production considerably.

It was now up to Number 1 Special Force to support the Partisan groups although the first task was to select which bands were true fighters and which were merely making warlike noises. It was also possible that the enemy had made bogus contacts in the hope of confusing British intelligence or even capturing agents.

Gradually as the weeks of planning and training passed, the Force began to send officers and men into the field to commence operations against the enemy. These men, dropped into enemy-occupied territory by parachute from Liberator, Halifax or Douglas DC-3 aeroplanes operating from Brindisi aerodrome, or even put ashore from submarines along the coast, began the work. Groups of operatives, varying in number according to the task allotted to them, were briefed, supplied and sent out. Tasks were many and varied. An Officer together with a wireless-operator would be dropped to help organise or to form Partisan units among the loyal Italian elements and then, once they had been fully established and contact had been made with base, would radio up supplies of food, arms and ammunition together with explosives, medical requirements etc.

Once equipped the bands could begin to harass the Germans in the rear areas and along their lines of communications. Other operations would involve small parties of men being dropped or landed with a definite target to attack, such as an important bridge or a busy section of railway track that would prove embarrassing if put out of action for any length of time. Anything in fact that would hinder the enemy was contemplated.

It was into this newly-established organisation that was now beginning to spread its wings in earnest, that Manfred Czernin arrived in November 1943. He naturally retained his Royal Air Force rank of Squadron Leader but as far as the Force was concerned he was just another officer sent from England to learn from scratch, the arts of waging war behind the enemy's lines. He soon fell into the swing of things along with other trainees, and was quickly taught the various secrets of his new profession. How to prepare explosives and plastic charges, where to place them in order to do the most damage, how to destroy railway terminals and bring down telegraph wires, how to kill an enemy soldier silently and effectively. All this had to be learnt to perfection, for one slip or one false move might mean capture for him and those men under his command. All agents were well aware of what that would mean!

It was also necessary for him to go through the parachute training course at the Force's Parachute School situated about two miles south of Monopoli. Although Manfred had already experienced a bale-out and a descent to earth by parachute, he was soon made aware of the vast difference between hurriedly leaving a doomed and burning Hurricane fighter during the heat of combat when the hands of death were reaching out, and the cold-blooded leap into space at night, loaded with equipment. There was also the task of learning about various Partisan bands he may have to deal with or work with. This in itself was no easy task for political allegiances of these groups were many and varied. Unless properly briefed, one could easily upset a particular group quite unwittingly by one wrong word. It was all very complex and the training exacting.

By the late autumn of 1943 the Battle for Italy was obviously not going as well for the Allies as had been hoped for. Following the Salerno landing the Allies had hoped for a speedy capture of Rome before the end of the year, but the Germans fought grimly and doggedly and this goal soon faded from view. With the approach of winter Partisan activity slowly ground to a halt, and those Italians for whom it was possible, dispersed to their homes, villages and farms to await the spring. For many others of course, it was not possible, having committed themselves as fighting patriots, leaving only one course of action open to them. In small groups they went into the high mountains or the forests to wait out the winter months. It was a grim prospect.

As the winter came to Italy the Allied front line stretched from the mouth of the River Carigliano on the Western Mediterranean coast, across the breadth of Italy to Ortona on the Adriatic coast. The obvious and immediate target north of this line was the Eternal City itself – Rome.

With the coming of spring, activity began to increase, both from the Partisans and the men of Number 1 Special Force. Even now the various resistance groups did not pose too much of a problem for the enemy but this would soon change during 1944. Manfred, by this time, had virtually completed his training and was eager to get into action. However, it was not just a case of being ready and then to go, everything had to fit into the overall plan, whatever his own specific mission might be.

As the first half of 1944 gradually drew on, Manfred became more and more impatient to get to work. Richard Hewitt, still second in command of the Force, remembers visiting Stefano Castle at about this time to find Manfred looking very morose and irritable at having not yet been selected to go north and get into action. Hewitt tried to reassure him that his turn would soon come, but he was probably not fully convinced, and he so very eager to get going.

Eventually his chance came, early in June and it came at a time when the Allied Armies reached and captured Rome. Manfred's mission was to lead a two-man team into the north-east area of Northern Italy, his companion being a small Bolognese man called Piero who would be his wireless operator.

For the next few days concise and detailed briefings were held. Both men studied maps of the area into which they would be dropped. All the latest information and intelligence was studied, such as which Partisan bands were known to be operating in the area and which enemy units they might have to encounter. False papers and documents were issued and the background biographies had to be committed to memory. Finally their equipment, especially Piero's radio with its spare parts, had to be prepared for the parachute drop. At last a date was set – June 12.

As the sky darkened that evening Manfred and Piero were driven to the airfield at Brindisi accompanied by Hedley Vincent, himself an SOE agent who had only recently returned from a mission in northern Italy. The men drove onto the field and pulled up outside the operations building. Little was said for it was a tense time for the two men about to be flown into enemy held territory. They put on their parachute harnesses, gathered their equipment together and with a final hand shake went out into the darkness. Climbing back into the jeep they drove across to the aeroplane that would transport them into danger. They stopped near the black shape of an American four-engined Liberator (B24) of the 15th Special Bomb Group, United States Army Air Force. It was now quite dark, only the dimmed lights from the aircraft's interior throwing an eerie glow from the entrance hatch. Their equipment aboard, they grabbed up their chest-type parachute packs, heaving them up at the crewman at the hatch. Piero climbed into the machine, helped by the crewman. Manfred was about to follow but as he went to do so, Vincent spotted Manfred's shoulder tapes.

'I say, Czernin, what's that on your shoulders?' Manfred knew he had been caught out, for instead of his Squadron Leader's rings, the pale blue and black shoulder tapes now indicated those of a Wing Commander.

'Oh come on, Hedley, what does it matter what rank I go in with?'

'You are a Squadron Leader and you'll go in as a Squadron Leader. Come on, change those tapes.'

Manfred was left with no choice but to comply and took down the Wing Commander's three tapes and replaced them with his proper ones. All this took some minutes but finally all was ready and Vincent slammed shut the hatch door after Manfred had climbed in. Cursing Manfred's indiscretion, he walked back to the operations building.

The big American Liberator's four engines were started up one by one, and Vincent watched as the aeroplane lumbered across the field to the runway. With a roar the throttles were pushed forward and the B24 gathered speed, rose majestically into the night sky and turned slowly northwards.

The darkened aeroplane made its way through the night sky to the most northern part of Italy, its destination being quite near to the Austrian frontier. Manfred and Piero said little to each other, each alone with his own thoughts. The months of training were now to be proved. In a few hours they could be among friendly Partisans – or they could be dead or prisoners. Even capture would probably mean death, for neither of them had any illusions about what would happen to them if taken. Although in uniform they would undoubtedly be shot. Already they knew of at least one agent who had been killed, having been tied up and run over by an armoured car. If the Gestapo thought an agent carried useful information death might be long and painful. The Liberator droned on into the night.

At last they reached their rendezvous point and the aeroplanes crewmen prepared the two men for the drop. Locating the dropping zone the pilot began to circle, looking down for the expected ground signals. Signals were seen but they were not those expected and reluctantly it was decided not to risk the jump. After checking with Manfred, the pilot turned the Liberator back onto a southerly course, heading the machine for Brindisi airfield. It was a maddening anti-climax to the months of preparation. Following a pensive 24 hour wait it was decided that they should try again and so once more the B24 took-off into the night sky of June 13, 1944.

This flight was even more nerve-racking for Manfred and Piero, for they knew that if they failed to make contact this time, the mission would be scrubbed altogether, and how long it might be before they would be chosen again, neither of them cared to guess. There was obviously a question of a possible trap laid by the Germans. Perhaps tonight they would spring it.

Once again the pilot located the dropping area and again he began to circle the B24. Manfred sat nervously waiting for the pilot to send back word that the ground signals had been seen, but yet again the signals were incorrect. What should he do? The obvious course was to go home but he could not bring himself to give the order, so the machine continued to circle while Manfred deliberated on what he should do. He looked across at Piero, then shouting above the noise of the engines, told the crewman to inform the pilot to make a dropping run. He was going in. Leaning forward he yelled into Piero's ear.

'I'm going to jump. If all is well, I'll give you the correct signal and you can then follow with the equipment. If I do not signal then go home.'

Piero nodded that he understood as the aeroplane turned onto its approach run. Manfred clipped on the parachute pack as the red light came on indicating that the drop area was coming up. Manfred sat with his legs over the escape hatch facing the rear of the aeroplane, his eyes fixed on the light panel. This was it, he thought. The only question now was were there friendly Italians below or unfriendly Germans. He was relaxed now,the waiting was over, he was back in action.

The green light flashed on and he felt the pressure of the crewman's hands on his shoulders as without another word or thought Manfred heaved himself down through the hatch into the dark abyss of the night. The sudden blast of the slipstream made him catch his breath, then he was falling. His parachute cracked open above his head and then all was quiet and still, the only sound being the fading roar of the Liberator's engines and the slight whistling breeze through the parachute lines.

Below lay the dark Italian landscape with the darker masses of the forest areas that abounded, and towards which he was fast approaching. He could just make out the clearing now and by pulling at the parachute's rigging lines as he had been taught, guided himself down towards it. Manfred hit the ground and rolled over. He was on his feet in a second, quickly gathering up the parachute lines and canopy.

Releasing the harness from his body he crouched down, his keen ears listening for any sound, his every sense alive to any danger. Shadows moved at the edge of the trees and he silently wished that he had brought a gun with him. He heard an Italian voice calling softly in the darkness. Well, he thought, it's not German but it could still be a trap. He stood up suddenly. If he was going to be shot it might as well be sooner as later.

A rapid burst of excited Italian language told him that he was among friends and the tension in his body relaxed. He was surrounded by a group of Partisans all shaking his hand and everyone was talking at once, but the sound of aero engines began to quieten them. The Liberator was coming back. Manfred told the Partisans to stay clear, then taking a flashlight from one of the men, he flashed the agreed signal up into the blackness. They heard the B24 go over and turn onto another run. Minutes later Piero, the guns and equipment was among them, Piero talking with relaxed excitedness in his native Bolognese tongue.

Now, however, it was time to move, for they had all been far too long in this one area while the aeroplane had circled around the dropping zone for some time. The leader of the band indicated the way, little being said as Manfred and Piero were taken through the wooded hillsides, then upwards into the mountains and forests.

Manfred's first mission behind the enemy's lines was mainly one of reconnaissance on the Austro-Italo frontier with the hope of penetrating into Austria itself. There was another mission in the area also, trying to do the same sort of thing, this mission being commanded by Major Fielding, whose code name was Rudolf. This other mission operated from Forni Avoitri and Sappade and were known as Force 133, which was later changed to Force 266, and later still to Force 399. This Force was also trying to operate into nearby Yugoslavia and Manfred's mission was just part of this main Force.

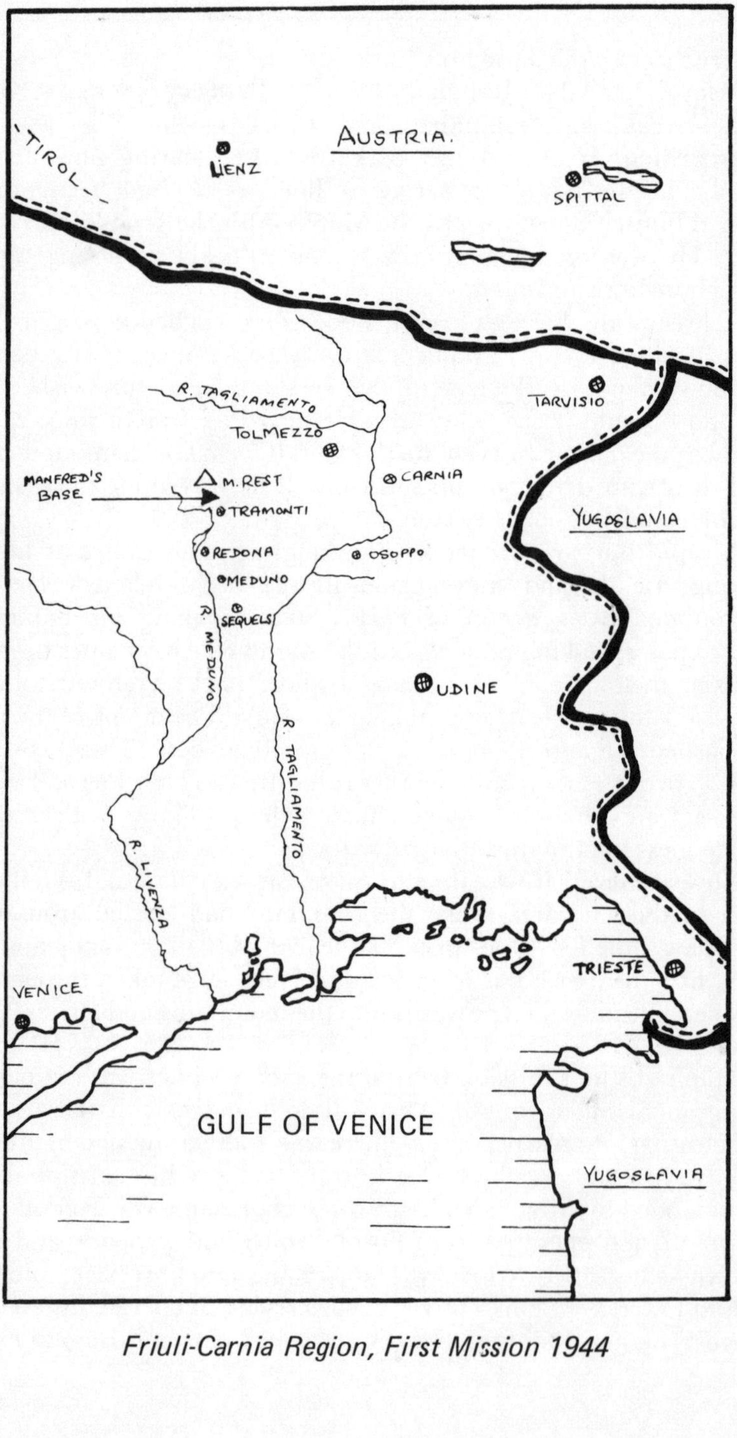

Friuli-Carnia Region, First Mission 1944

Even at this stage of the war Yugoslav Partisans were on occasions fighting the Italian Garibaldi Partisan group as well as the common German enemy, and it soon appeared to Manfred that a part of his job would be to try and keep these rival factions away from each other as much as possible.

Manfred made his base in a farm house at a small village called Tramonti di Sopra. The farm nestled at the foot of a large mountain named Monto Rest; in fact the whole area of Tramonti was a relatively small table-top plateau, surrounded by high mountains with picturesque streams meandering across the flat pastureland, running down from the higher regions of the mountains. While it was an almost perfect place for a base it did have its disadvantages, for its high mountains made it dangerous for aeroplanes to make low level dropping runs and the streams and sometimes marshy ground would make supply drops wasteful.

Tramonti di Sopra was a group of only a few houses and farm buildings with a comparatively small population. Manfred's farm house was situated at the northern end of the village and it was here that he and Piero prepared their plans. From this vantage point they could look down on the plateau as well as the larger villages of Tramonti di Mezzo and Tramonti di Sotto. At Tramonti, Manfred soon made contact with his British liaison officer, another SOE officer, Pat Martin-Smith, whom the Italians called 'Maggiore Pat'. It was not long before Piero had set up his radio, and had made contact with base. Then he and Manfred began to settle down in their mountain home and began to think of the immediate future.

The area in which Tramonti was situated was controlled in the main by the Communist-led Garibaldi Partisans, and with whom Manfred was to work and co-operate. After making contact and finding their immediate needs, he radioed base and arranged for supplies and equipment to be flown in. There followed a period of instruction, during which time he passed on to the Partisans his knowledge of the preparation and use of explosives, fuses, etc: Then it became a question of to what use this should be put. The railway system in the Carnia region was an obvious target and Manfred collaborated in several attacks on that system. This railway which ran through Carnia eventually made its way down to important towns such as Trieste and Venice as well as Udine, Gorisia and Treviso. It is not difficult to imagine a typical expedition to attack a section of railway line.

The locality would be chosen with care and then reconnoitred well in advance. Train times and likely enemy patrols would be noted, then when all was ready, explosives would be prepared and then men selected for the job. In the late afternoon the Partisans would begin to make their way across country through the woods and valleys, reaching their destination at about dusk or just after. All would be quiet as they scrambled down an embankment, then silently they would creep across to the silver tracks gleaming in the night light. They would stop at intervals and listen, every sound of the night being examined in case an enemy patrol was near. When they had planted their deadly charges, with other Partisans covering their colleagues, fingers gently caressing the triggers of their sub-machine guns and rifles. All completed, they would then disappear into the trees, set off the charges, and quickly make their way back to base.

Manfred and his group were attacked by enemy forces on at least three occasions and each time he lost practically all his equipment, but each time he managed to evade capture. The vastness of the northern Italian mountain regions made it almost impossible for the Germans or the Fascists to police it adequately although in Manfred's area of operations, the ill-famed Cossacks, had, from time to time, to be avoided.

During the early months of his mission, Manfred managed to penetrate across the border into Austria and did eventually manage to establish two lines across the frontier, which made coming and going between the two countries much easier, and the lines could also be used for bringing out political refugees etc: Although it was hoped that some contact might be made with Austrian patriots and possible Partisan units, this was never successfully accomplished, either by Manfred or anybody else.

Manfred's Tramonti base in the Friuli region of North East Italy was situated approximately 40 kilometres from the Austrian border and about 50 kilometres from the Yugoslavian frontier. The nearest large towns were Tolmezzo to the north east and Belluno to the west. A road ran from Udine, the provincial capital down on the plains, 50 kilometres to the south east, and this road eventually wound its way through Sequels into the mountains at a place called Meduno then up to and through Tramonti, via Redona with its beautiful lake, following the River Meduna after leaving Sequels. After Tramonti and the plateau land, the road went around the foot of Monte Rest, winding down the valleys to cross the River Tagliamento to join the Carnia-Tolmezzo-Ampezzo road. This latter section going through the narrow mountain passes, was blown up in several places by the Partisans and in fact was not fully repaired until 1960.

During one of Manfred's excursions, he and Piero took shelter and rest in a small, empty, half ruined mediaeval watch tower high up in the mountains. Early the next morning they heard, and then saw, a troop of German soldiers marching up towards the tower. The two men were high up in the tower but some Partisans who were with them and who had slept on the lower floor managed to get away into the woods, but Manfred and Piero were unable to get away in time. The Germans arrived and began to make camp around the tower, the officers settling down in the lower hall recently vacated by the Italians.

Manfred and his companion were completely cut off and had no choice but to stay quiet and pray that the Germans would not decide to explore the upper part of the tower.

Shutting themselves into a small room at the top, they sat on the floor for twelve long hours, with loaded revolvers in their hands pointing to the door. After this long and seemingly never-ending wait, to their immense relief, they eventually heard the soldiers being paraded out in front of the tower – it was now sunset. The two men quickly took this chance, swiftly making their way down the steps of the tower and escaped through a rear door. Within seconds they made their dash across the clearing, keeping the tower between them and the Germans, and soon they were swallowed up in the fir trees just as the sun disappeared behind the mountains.

All the various adventures he went through during the period June to November 1944 may never be fully known, and his own romantic stories did little to give a really clear picture. For instance he is supposed to have shot one of his Partisan band who, although warned repeatedly, continued to maltreat a German prisoner. For the sake of maintaining his discipline and position he had to take the law into his own hands on this occasion.

Another story is that for a brief period he was captured. While there appears to be no official report of this incident, it would be just like Manfred to say nothing of it to his superiors, in case they should take him out of action which would naturally preclude him from any chance of seeing further action on other missions. He told the story after the war to his friend Hiram Smith, with whom it will be remembered he had been at 52 OTU in 1941. He also told his mother the same story, to whom he never in his life romanticised any of his adventures!

It happened apparently, during one of his forays across the frontier into Austria, and probably he was only in custody, under suspicion, for a short while. Somehow he was picked up and taken to a house for questioning, but his fluent Italian gave no hint that he was English, but his captors may have suspected him of being a Partisan. He was beaten up several times by his captors, most of whom were Austrian soldiers, and he felt sure that he was not going to be allowed to live through it. He then overheard an officer saying that they would take him to Trieste, but he then had an opportunity to escape. Only one German guard stood between him and freedom for a few minutes. It was now or never. Manfred got away – the German died.

Some credence to this story can be imagined and his rapid escape understood when it is realised that in nearby Trieste he had an Austrian cousin of the same family name. This cousin held a post in the German SS. Once face to face with him, which may have easily happened, the game would have most certainly been up.

In September 1944 he had company in his mountain village when two more Special Force Officers were parachuted down near his locality. They were Major Tom Rowarth, who was to take charge of the area, and his second-in-command, Captain Richard Tolson. Although it had been originally planned for them to operate nearer the Yugoslavian frontier, it was found that their briefing had not been too thorough and so they moved north west to Tramonti. Pat Martin-Smith brought Manfred to Rowarth and introduced him to the new area commander. During their ensuing conversation, Manfred was able to confirm that it was the Garibaldini Partisans who controlled the district and not the group he had been briefed to expect. Rowarth had to make a quick decision and decided to support the Communist group and establish his mission in the area.

By this time, Manfred's main task had been completed and he was at something of a loose end. Also the winter was approaching. Being a person who always needed action and things to do, and now having little of both he started to become a bit of a nuisance and was, along with others, leaning heavily on Rowarth's mission to get supply drops, especially because he had lost practically all his main equipment during enemy attack, as already related.

Finally it was decided that Manfred should return to base and shortly afterwards, Rowarth signalled base to fly up an aircraft to pick him up. On October 29, a single-engined Westland Lysander III of Special Air Service, flew into the mountain base at Tramonti di Mezzo. After his good-byes to the Italians with whom he had lived and fought for four months, the 'Lizzie' took off. Manfred looked back with some sadness at the valleys and mountains that had been his home and base during the summer of 1944.

Piero remained behind, going over to Rowarth's mission. Shortly after Manfred's return to the SOE base, now situated at Siena, came the order to suspend the dropping of agents into enemy territory until the spring. At the same time came the news of big enemy *restrallamentos* (German and Fascist sweeps into Partisan-held territories). The Cossacks over-ran Tramonti during one sweep, forcing Rowarth to go to ground while Richard Tolson left him to join another mission.

These enemy sweeps had in fact started in a small way during September, after the Allied Command had ordered Partisan groups in the Venetia area to sabotage all main roads and hold the Alpine passes, thinking that the Germans were about to retreat. However, they did not retreat, but instead, strongly attacked their immediate antagonists, putting several Partisan bands to flight during their *restrallamentos*, executing prisoners without ceremony and burning villages whose residents were suspected of assisting or supporting local Partisans.

One example of the enemy's ruthless attacks was on Monti Grappa in Venetia, just north of Bassano, where some 1,700 Partisans were concentrated. This group attacked German units in the area but were vigorously counter-attacked. Seven hundred Partisans were captured and of these 264 were shot. Certain Partisan groups showed more than usual courage, one group being the Red Star Brigade under Mario Musolesi, known among the men of the resistance as 'Maggiore Lupo'.

This band of some two hundred men were based around Monti Sole and Monti Salvaro, situated between the Reno and Setta Rivers on the route from Florence to Bologna. They accomplished a great deal of harassment and were brave and resolute fighters. Musolesi did so much damage to the Germans that the 16th Panzer Division was ordered up to wipe them out completely. Led by Major Walter

Reder, a veteran of the French, Russian and Yugoslavian fronts, the Division attacked, pursued and wiped out the band on September 29, Musolesi being killed alongside his gallant men. Many local civilians around the Monti Sole area were also taken and killed without mercy.

Returning from his first mission behind enemy lines, Manfred was recommended for the Military Cross for his work and courage, especially when taking the decision to parachute down when the reception signals had not been either clear or accurate. The award was approved and Gazetted on December 1, 1944.

After de-briefing and a rest, Manfred was made a Despatch Officer which allowed him to move about reasonably freely in his beloved Italy, south of the lines that is, and he was able to spend leave periods at Ravello. His mother's house, the lovely 'Swallow's Nest' was, with Manfred's permission, used as a rest centre for the men of No 1 Special Force during the latter part of the war. It did, for a while, take away all thoughts of war from the men's weary minds and bodies. With the beautiful gardens of the villa together with the view across the Bay of Sorrento, it was very easy to be at rest and forget the war.

As a Despatch Officer he managed to get hold of a motor-cycle to travel from place to place, soon getting the hang of this mode of travel which he had not used since his youth. He often travelled at high speed for the sheer exhilaration of using the machine's power. On one occasion he was travelling to a mountain headquarters when an Italian asked if he would be kind enough to give him a lift. Manfred agreed and the man settled himself upon the pillion seat. The HQ was situated at the very top of a long winding, twisting road and Manfred roared up and around the curves with mountain side to the right and a sheer drop to the left. The poor Italian clung to Manfred like grim death, eventually falling off in a dead faint when at last they reached the top.

Now, however,the winter had arrived and the year of 1945 was soon to dawn.

At about this time, Manfred returned to England for a brief rest and in fact ran into his old friend Hiram Smith. Hiram recalls:

'It was not until the autumn of 1944 that I met Manfred again. I had returned to England (from India) to go to a Fighter Leader School course at Millfield and happened to run into him in London.

We spent several hectic days and nights on the town! It was then that I found out that he was in the cloak and dagger business but I must say he was very reticent about what he had been doing. We met up with a big Scandinavian who was also in the same line of business and rather more talkative, but nevertheless little was disclosed. No doubt a pity in retrospect but at the time it was obviously imprudent to probe very much. I did ask Manfred, however, why he had gone into special agent work but the only reason he gave was that he had become bored with life in India. This may not be the main reason but one who enjoyed civilised life, companionship and amenities as much as Manfred did, would have found squadron life on a jungle airstrip in Bengal distinctly unrewarding.'

Several points emerge from this meeting with Hiram Smith at the end of 1944, bearing in mind what is now known of Manfred's personality. The first point is that Manfred apparently made little or no mention of his work in Italy which in some respects is strange when one recalls that he was often known to let people know what he was doing and even to embellish the truth for effect. This reluctance to talk about his special work is confirmed by Maud who admits that Manfred told her nothing of what he had been doing other than it was of a secret nature. Again strange as by this time Manfred had the ribbon of the Military Cross sewn next to his DFC ribbon, as is shown in a magazine clipping of the couple, taken as always in a Mayfair restaurant during an evening out, and one can assume he was asked to explain how he had earned this by all manner of people and friends.

His reasons for joining SOE are known but the reasons he gave Hiram are a little more like the real Manfred, preferring to admit that it was boredom, rather than age and near-breakdown in health that made operational flying no longer possible. Although one understands the Wing Commander's comments on what Manfred liked, life behind enemy lines cannot have been very 'civilised' nor could the amenities have been that luxurious. Altogether a most interesting if modest conversation from the Count. He could have spun quite a yarn to his old friend.

In ending this chapter of Manfred's life, and the end of his story about his first mission behind enemy lines let one more story be related, a story Manfred told his friend Alwyn Bolton. It concerns the occasion when Manfred visited a nearby town and decided to kill some time by visiting a cinema. Apparently, when the interval came and the lights went up, he found himself sitting next to a German Officer. The German became quite talkative and in the ensuing conversation enquired as to Manfred's nationality. Manfred, smiling, turned to the German and said he was British. At this the German suddenly roared with laughter, thinking this remark highly amusing!

CHAPTER NINE

Special Operations
The Second Mission

By the late autumn of 1944 it had become only too apparent that the Allied Armies in Italy would be able to make little further progress in the campaign during the coming winter months. General Alexander, Commander-in-Chief of the British Forces engaged in Italy, had at this time to issue orders and instructions to the Partisans in the north, outlining the role that they were to play during the next few months.

Alexander's first instruction to them was the task of reducing to a minimum their numbers and, as in the previous winter of 1943-44, those who could, should return to their homes. This, it was hoped, would help those who had no choice but to remain in the hills, woods and mountains, to keep alive on the limited food supplies that they had and the limited supplies that could be dropped to them. All large-scale sabotage and attack actions were to cease although small harassing operations should continue whenever a situation presented itself.

Following a halt during November, British Liaison Officers (BLO's) were again parachuted into the north and the existing missions already in the field were of course maintained. The BLO's immediate task was to keep alive the Partisan movement over the difficult winter period, a task which took a great deal of diplomacy and tact. Those Partisan groups that remained in the mountains suffered severe hardships during this period from both weather and shortage of food, and while they were in this weakened state, the enemy continued to make strong attacks upon them. Early in the new year of 1945, several allied divisions were transferred from Italy to the Western Front, and this naturally reduced the forces that would eventually be required to continue the offensive in the spring, and who would be needed to maintain law and order in Northern Italy later, which in turn would mean an even greater Partisan effort to ensure success of the final assault on the north by Allied forces.

This development came at a time when Partisan morale was particularly low, following many arrests of patriots in towns and cities in the North. This had naturally disorganised much of the clandestine work in both the cities and the plains. In some instances, organisations had had to be dissolved completely. To give some indication of the losses sustained by the Partisans, General Karl Wolff, Commander of the German SS in Italy, stated that some 80,000 Partisans had been disarmed and captured, with an additional 9,000 killed, in one three month period. While these figures may have been exaggerated for propaganda purposes, actual Partisan losses were still very high.

In late January 1945, Allied Forces Headquarters in Italy, rapidly began to increase deliveries of food, clothing, arms and explosives, directing the Partisans to concentrate on as much sabotage and harassing activities as possible. Abnormally good weather during February enabled these supplies to be increased even more. The American Air Force squadrons of the 15th Special Bomb Group, flying B24 Liberators and later named the 2641st Special Bomb Group, together with the C47s of the 62nd TC Group (later replaced by the 64th Group) flew the majority of these sorties, from bases at Brindisi, Malignano (near Siena) and Rosignano, near Cecina. The Liberators were flown on all night missions, while the C47s flew on daylight supply drops escorted by fighters.

This increased activity and the regular supplies helped to encourage the Partisans to reform their groups quickly in the early spring, and in spite of earlier setbacks, it seemed hopeful at AFHQ that a 'D-Day' date (already hoped for during April) might be realised. During these early months something like 170 tons of arms and 70 tons of explosives, together with 70 tons of other equipment, were dropped into the north-west area alone.

Time was now short for the planned April target date and it was, therefore essential that the British missions already in operation should be both reinforced and increased in number. This policy resulted in 59 British Officers and 66 other ranks being sent in, and established in, these northern areas by April 1, 1945, in addition to

92 Italian agents recruited and trained in Italy by No 1 Special Force.

One of these British officers sent in was Squadron Leader Manfred Czernin, MC, DFC. Again all preliminary preparations were made and briefings held. He was as eager as ever to get back into action and was pleased to have been chosen once again to go into the north. As soon as the orders came through to No 1 Special Force, via SOMTO (Subversive Operations in the Mediterranean Theatre Office), under the command of General Stawell, he was back on top of the world. By March 21 he and his team were ready. That evening they were driven to the airfield outside Siena where an American Liberator stood waiting.

For this mission Manfred had four men under his command. His second in command was Lieutenant Giuliano Mattioli, a strikingly tall, fair-haired, good-looking Italian, who had been educated at Harrow School. As well as assisting Manfred, Mattioli's specific job was to help protect the Dams in the area of the operation, from destruction by retreating enemy troops. For some time he had been studying the location, disposition and defences of these Dams and had detailed plans for their protection. The third man in the party was another Italian whom they called 'Moicano' (Mohican). He was the armament and explosives expert and also an aggressive, competent soldier. Big, solid and dark, he was a man not to be trifled with in any situation, or by anyone. Several of the enemy found this out to their cost. The remaining two in the team were British NCOs who were the wireless-operators.

Giuliano Mattioli, for whom this was to be his fourth mission into enemy-held territory, felt a little disturbed as the car drove up to the big Liberator, as he then discovered that the pilot who was to fly them deep into and behind the enemy lines, was only 19 years of age!

The five men climbed in and made themselves comfortable amid the large amount of supplies that would be dropped with them. Taking-off the B24 headed north towards the Swiss border, the five men each sitting with his own thoughts of the immediate future. Finally they were nearing the drop zone and the pilot radioed to the crewman to get the men and supplies ready. The time of waiting was again at an end.

Manfred and his four men, followed by their equipment, were dropped among the sharp peaks of the Mortirollo Alpine Massif.

They landed near the town of Tirano just south of the Swiss border between the two villages of Val Tirano and Incudine where their Italian Partisan reception committee were waiting for them.

Manfred's main task during this mission was to co-ordinate the various scattered Partisan units in the Bergamasco District, into a unified command and with these co-ordinated forces, to carry out the orders and directives of the 15th Army Group. Not being absolutely certain of the exact location, or disposition of the Partisans in this area it had been previously decided to drop Manfred and his team in this more northerly area and leave them to make their way south-west towards the town of Bergamo. From the local Tirano Partisans, Manfred purchased some mules onto which they loaded their supplies of arms, ammunition, food and even Bazooka anti-tank weapons, etc: and began to make their way across country and over the mountains towards the village of Aprica, by night march.

It was hard going, but by dawn they reached the outskirts of the village and looked about for a place to stop and rest before deciding how and when to carry on. By this time Manfred's feet had become swollen and bruised by the march and were giving him some trouble. A quick reconnaissance of the route ahead, showed an open valley and as the sun was now rising, it was decided that they should stay under cover and out of sight, not attempting to cross the open valley in daylight.

Manfred then decided that if they were going to stay in the locality, he would go down into the village with the intention of seeking medical treatment for his feet. Mattioli earnestly warned him against this course of action, for they had previously been warned that the area was dangerous for in the village was not only a German garrison but also had a detachment of German railway technicians.

Manfred, nevertheless, with his usual disregard for personal danger, strolled down into the village accompanied by Moicano, leaving the other three well hidden in a hayrick. On reaching the village, Manfred and Moicano openly sauntered through the main street and into a tavern full of German soldiers. The Germans were all singing and had obviously just finished an early breakfast, starting the working day well. Some discreet words to the owner of the tavern and the two men were quickly but quietly, whisked upstairs and out of sight. Manfred then talked the tavern owner into

Mario Invernicci, Zone Commander with the XXIV May partisan group of the G.L. (Liberation Group) Division. With Manfred he shared the dangers and the triumphs of the liberation of the Provincial town of Bergamo.

(Below) Manfred, with gun slung over right shoulder, speaking to the people of Bergamo and the Partisan Forces in the first days after the liberation. To his immediate left (with glasses) is Colonel Morley Fletcher MC, the Allied Commissioner in the Bergamo area.

Avro Anson (G-AJHK) shortly before Manfred and two friends left for Johannesburg to start an air freight business in May 1947.

The family man. Manfred with his children Carolyn and Nicholas, 1950.

Warrior's Rest. The temple at Villa Cimbrone, Ravello, where Manfred's ashes lie. In the land of his childhood, the country he loved.

attending to his feet. So there sat Manfred in an upstairs room, bathing his feet while listening to the Germans enjoying themselves below, with Moicano standing by the door, his pistol in his hand.

Fully refreshed,the two men later returned to the three others, and they waited for sundown. Loading up the mules once more they crossed the open valley and now ahead of them was the 9,000 foot high Passo del Diaviolo, which they found completely covered with snow, in places being up to six feet deep. The spring weather was beginning to melt the mountain snow and ice and it was soon found that the mules, with their heavy loads, were sinking. It became apparent that they would only be able to get the supplies across the Pass if they were carried by hand. Manfred, therefore, called upon the local villagers and hired just over twenty people for the task. These inhabitants of the villages near the Swiss frontier were already happily engaged, so they understood, in various smuggling activities between Italy and Switzerland and they had to be carefully watched while handling such valuable merchandise.

Having gathered together his band of hired help, Manfred moved forward up the mountain tracks but they were soon forced back by the intense cold and the ever-present danger of landslides and avalanches from the melting ice. After another full day of hiding they tried again and this time they managed to get about half way up before being forced to halt. This time they discovered a disused shepherd's hut where they stashed the arms, and while Manfred and his followers returned to the lower slopes, Mattioli stayed alone in the hut to guard the equipment. He remained there for two days, then on the second night, Manfred and the others returned, determined this time to succeed in making the crossing. Luck then took a hand, for a sudden cold spell temporarily halted the spring thaw. Marching off at 0400 am on the morning of April 4, Manfred led his band across the Pass and after marching in the bitter cold continuously for twenty-four hours, all suffering from frost-bite, cold and lack of food, they finally succeeded in making the other side.

Manfred paid off his helpers then took refuge in an old construction hut that pre-war builders of a nearby dam had used. They had half expected some sort of reception party from the Bergamasco region Partisans but for the whole of the first day they saw no one. On the following day they saw a large column of people slowly making their way up the mountain towards them. Looking through field glasses, they recognised German uniforms. Manfred and his men, barracaded the door, preparing to defend themselves, when they suddenly noticed some oddly dressed men, also some women and several animals. It transpired that the column was a group of deserting Russian soldiers who had been pressed into German service rather than suffer the horrors of a prison camp. Local Partisans, not knowing what to do with three hundred or so Russians, their women, children and animals, had promised to lead them to the Swiss frontier. It was thus, that contact was made by the Special Force men with the Partisans of the Bergamasco and the Val Brembana.

The beautiful Val Brembana, situated some 15 miles north of Bergamo, was a very pleasant location in which to stay, especially now that spring was in the air, as well as being a base one could easily defend. High up in the surrounding mountains the Partisans could look down into the narrow green valley that occasionally opened out into pleasant basins where, here and there, caves could be seen and also the curious two-coloured chalk strata in the rock and hillsides. The River Brembo gently flowed alongside the valley road which had been cut out of the chalk, leaving it at the Villa D'Àlma, just north of Bergamo, to join the River Adda which runs from Lecco to the Po.

As always, Manfred's forceful character captured the imagination of those under his command. To them, he was impressively tall with handsome features and blond good looks, which everyone took to be typically English. To the Partisans he was soon known as 'Maggiore Manfredi' and he would often be seen riding his horse, which was the usual mode of travel in this part of the mountains, over the steep slopes of the Partisan mountain headquarters. One of his young officers was an 18 year old second lieutenant, Dominic Flessati, known by his Partisan name of 'Borbolo'.

At this time, young Flessati was struck by Manfred's courtesy, even in moments of great stress, and even to very junior subordinates such as himself. During one encounter with the Germans Flessati lost his gun, but Manfred immediately gave him his own.

Manfred's Bergamasco area in the north-west, was part of the area known as the Lombardy Sector. It comprised several groups of Partisans under a Zone Command. The Leader of the Zone was a man named, or rather known as, 'Bassi', based in Bergamo Province with an estimated 1,000 Partisans of mixed political loyalties. There were also about 600 Partisans of the Action Party in the 'Olona' Group of the G L Division (Liberation Group). These men were under the command of a leader named Marcello and were all based in and around the valleys of Brembana, Sereana and Cavallina. In addition there was a Fiamme Verdi (Green Flames) Group under Alberto, in which Dominic Flessati served. These numbered about 100 men all based in the Val Taleggio. Lastly there was the strong Communist Garibaldini Group of some 300 men in the Val Taleggio and the Val Cavallina areas. In general each Partisan band or group was called a Brigade, both to flatter the leaders and also to deceive the enemy as to the exact strength of the groups. The average strength of a brigade was between three and four hundred armed men. A number of Brigades would be controlled overall by a *Commando Unico*.

To fully understand and appreciate the many and varied political (or even non-political) allegiances of the Partisan Groups would take a volume by itself, and it is not the intention of this book to discuss these aspects in any detail. As mentioned in the previous chapter, Manfred's first mission was mainly among the Communist Garibaldini Groups of the North East region in the Venetia Sector. To give some idea to the reader of the background of the Partisan formations in Occupied Italy, it might help to know how the movement was made up politically.

A more or less accurate break-down as a percentage of the total Partisan organisation could be listed as follows:

35.25%	—	Communist
27.75%	—	Non political
14.00%	—	Not known
11.00%	—	Action Party (GL)
10.50%	—	Christian Democrat (Fiamme Verdi)
1.50%	—	Socialist
100.00%		

In France the various French Resistance movement were also involved to a certain degree in political allegiances within their groups, but on the whole, they decided to drop political aims in order to concentrate their total energies against the common enemy – the Germans. The Italian Partisans, however, seemed to have as much inter-group trouble as they had battles with the Germans and

Fascists. If a Christian Democrat band appeared to get more help and supplies from parachute drops, than, shall we say, a Communist group, mass arguments and intense rivalry would develop and the British Liaison Officers in charge of the various units involved, had much of their time taken up in sorting out these problems, as well as trying to fight the enemy.

In Manfred's Lombardy Sector, there were an estimated 13,000 Partisans made up politically as follows:

total men:	3,100	——	Non political	=	23%
	2,200	——	Communist	=	18%
	1,700	——	Action Party	=	14%
	3,862	——	Christian Democrat	=	29%
	2,150	——	Not known	=	16%
					100%

Manfred had, therefore, the additional task of keeping these groups as contented and well-supplied as he could as well as trying to unify them into one complete formation. Those arms which he and his team had brought with them were distributed by himself and Mattioli as well as arranging subsequent drops that were organised on his radioed instructions via his radio operators. It was fortunate that his high degree of diplomacy in these matters proved adequate in keeping everyone satisfied. For the first two or three weeks after crossing the Passo del Diaviolo, Manfred and Mattioli toured the district, supplying and distributing arms and ammunition to the groups and setting up his general overall organisation, from his base near Zogno, itself an enemy garrison town.

The Allied date for D-Day in Northern Italy was set for April 5, 1945, which was the beginning of the 15th British Army Group's spring offensive. The American 5th Army was also involved in this drive northwards. Opposing the Allied forces were 16 German and Fascist Divisions of the 10th and 14th Armies, in a line approximately 40 miles north of Florence. Briefly, the German 10th Army line commenced 15 miles north of Ravenna on the Adriatic Coast where the 76th Panzer Corps held the line from the sea, inland to the Via Emilia. Here the 1st Parachute Corps continued the line westward to just east of Route 65, and here the 14th Army took over, with the 14th Panzer Corps holding the line westwards to Vergato. From Vergato the 51st Mountain Corps took the line to the

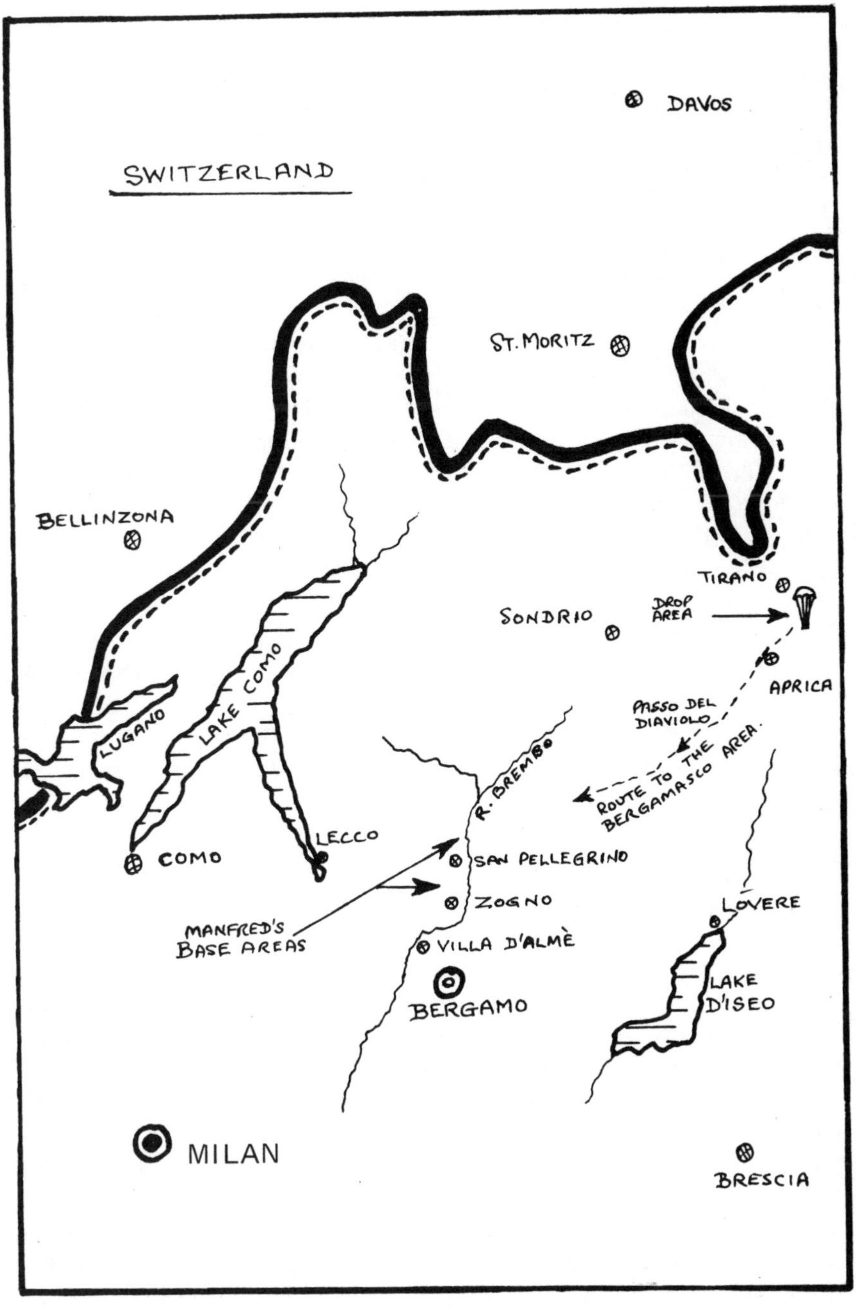

Bergamo Area, Second Mission 1945

Mediterranean Coast, 20 miles to the south of Spezia.

The remainder of Northern Italy was held, in the north-east, in the Trieste-Udine-Venice area, by the 73rd and 79th German Corps, and in the Lombardy region there was the Army Liguria, together with the Corps Lombardy and the 75th Corps. In the Aosta region in the far north-west were four regiments of the Littorio Division with some German units, while in the central sector at Paicenza, which was about 40 miles south of Bergamo, was the 1st Italian SS Infantry Division.

The Allied advance was, in the main, surprisingly rapid from the offset. The British 8th Army advanced rapidly up to and through the Argenta Gap then onwards to the River Po. The British 5th Army, after some stiff initial opposition, swept through the Apennines and on to Verona, where the Adige Line was turned, suddenly making the way open to the Brenner Pass, Austria, Venice, Udine and Trieste.

Due to the rapid advance of the Allied thrusts, the Germans were only able to mount one drive against the Partisans, who were being particularly active. This drive took place in the north-west region, in the locality of Cigliano-Tronzano. It was believed to have been planned in order to keep the autostrada from Turin open so that the withdrawal of the German 75th Corps to Como could take place without opposition. In this attempt some 2,000 troops, 400 vehicles and armour, were employed and were thus tied down away from the front line.

No sooner were the Apennines cleared of enemy positions than the Allied Command gave the 'All Out' order to attack the north-west regions and the 92nd American Division advanced from Genoa, which had already been liberated by local Partisan forces. The Americans then began to advance along the coast westwards to Savona, where they then turned north and west towards Turin. Meanwhile, the 4th Corps advanced on Verona and onwards towards the provincial town of Bergamo.

In the Bergamasco area things began to happen in mid-April when on the 25th the Partisan GL Divison headed by the Zone Commissar Mario Invernicci, cleared the Val Brembana, under their BLO, Manfred Czernin. This began when the order for 'All Out' action against the enemy was received and the Partisans ur der Manfred, stormed down from their mountain strongholds in the upper Val Brembana. His forces quickly over-ran three enemy garrisons, while he and the rest of his group moved towards the three larger towns in his immediate area.

The first town to receive his Partisan attentions was Zogno, the nearest to his base. On the evening of the 25th, Manfred decided, in conjunction with Mario Invernicci, to move with the XXIV MAY Partisan formation, towards Bergamo, sending messages to other Partisan units to do the same. The decisive factor was the news, received from the city, that their comrades in Bergamo, having taken occupation of the Town Hall, found themselves in rather a critical situation. At that very moment, in fact, in addition to German troops already garrisoned in the city under the command of SS Unterstürmführer Langen, in company with several black-shirted Fascist brigades, led by the ill-famed Resmini, there were several retreating German units passing through Bergamo.

Added to this situation was the unofficial news reporting that a German surrender had been signed, which made the German commanders uncertain as to what they should do. With the Germans being urgently pressed by the Bergamo CLN (National Liberation Committee), and by Bruno Quarti of the CVL (Voluntary Liberation Committee) to leave the city, it is easy to imagine how delicate the general situation of the Bergamo Partisans had become now that they had played their hand and come out into the open. The general overall chaos of the moment did not help matters.

Access to the provincial town would not of course be easy, and it would be a great mistake to under-estimate the Fascist garrisons stationed between Serina and Bergamo, the two main ones being Zogno and San Pellegrino. There was every indication that these well-armed bases would make an all-out effort to cut the Partisans off. In addition to obvious political antagonism, these Fascists also feared that the Partisans would take severe revenge for their many comrades who had lost their lives in previous clashes with the hated Fascists.

The danger of an armed collision, with not only the unavoidable loss of life on both sides, would delay the Partisans reaching Bergamo. Manfred and Invernicci had to consider their plan of action very carefully, which was far from easy since they also had to curb the not unnatural urge of their men to storm the garrisons and kill everyone they found. Having calculated all the possibilities, Invernicci decided to get in touch with the Commander of the Fascist GNR (National Republican Guard), by telephone, at Zogno.

Having made the contact, Invernicci informed the Commander that the town was completely surrounded by his Partisans, and that shortly the Zone Commissar, himself, and the Allied Major Manfredi, would call on him to negotiate surrender terms. The Fascist Commander was also informed that during these negotiations, they would keep in touch with their Partisan forces and that any interruption of these communications would be interpreted as meaning that Manfred and Mario were in danger. This would bring down the main Partisan body to the barracks where they had orders to shoot all the occupants.

After the telephone conversation, final arrangements were made with the XXIV MAY Commander, Renato (whose real name was Fortunato Fasana) and Adriano (real name Adriano de Vecchi) on what action they should take in case of any aggression on the part of the Fascist garrison. This decided upon, Manfred and Mario went into the town and presented themselves, not without some trepidation, at the Fascist barracks.

They found the Commander's office situated on the first floor of one of the buildings, and at the end of a long dark staircase. They climbed the stairs, sub-machine-guns in their hands, having already noticed that more or less all the GNR men had made themselves scarce. In his office the Commander sat surrounded by a group of his young officers, from whose faces Manfred could read a natural uneasiness of the situation. It was likely that the GNR men feared instant retaliation for their past acts, and that the two Partisan leaders were about to announce what their fate would be. Manfred and Mario stood squarely in front of the Fascist group, both parties feeling like the mouse in a cat and mouse game. Then with appropriate firmness, Manfred demanded, as representatives of the National Liberation Committee and the British Government, unconditional surrender of the garrison, its men and its arms.

'You will also,' continued Manfred to the Commander, 'be fully responsible for the conduct of your men and any insubordination on their part.'

At once some of the officers began to refuse categorically to accept any form of peaceful solution, pulling out their pistols and revolvers, pointing them at the two men, gesticulating wildly. Mario quickly called upon the Commander for order, telling him to be less of a fool and to be more realistic.

'Can't you see you have no choice? You are surrounded and any hostility on your part will only lead to needless bloodshed.' The officers, however, continued to refuse surrender, preferring to fight it out, rather than just submit meekly. It was a tense moment while the Commander weighed up the situation. Manfred slowly moved his hand and released the safety catch on his machine-gun. The Commander, being unable to seek advice from his superiors, was torn between dramatic uncertainty and the fear generated by his officers. In fact the central Fascist command at Bergamo would not now reply to any of the Commander's calls and this feeling of complete isolation also affected the officers. Finally the Commander declared himself willing to submit but refused to give a written statement to Manfred to this effect. However, he and Mario accepted a de-facto unconditional surrender, leaving the men free to go after they had first handed over their arms before vacating the barracks.

Manfred and Mario were more pleased to have avoided the use of arms in the surrender, each heartily congratulating the other on their success.

There was now the question of the spa town of San Pellegrino where there was a strong detachment of the hostile *Milizia Forestale* (Forestry Militia), who were well armed and under the command of a full Colonel. The Partisans had already had several clashes with this garrison at the beginning of December 1944 when the *Milizia* made a sudden and brutal *restrallamento* through the Dossena, Serina and Mount Alben localities, which resulted in the death of five Partisans. Due to this episode which as far as the Partisans were concerned had been extremely serious, there was no love lost for these Militiamen. These men in fact belonged to a special corps and could perfectly well have refused to take part in the Sweep. They were, therefore, quite fearful of Partisan revenge at this particular time.

The XXIV MAY formation quickly occupied the town and then with equal haste moved on and surrounded the barracks of the garrison. Again it was Manfred and Mario who went forward to negotiate surrender terms. It was a quick and less tense business than the previous confrontation, because the news of the surrender of the GNR at Zogno had already been received. The Militiamen silently handed over their arms in the barrack yard. Since many of these men had their families lodging in rooms near the barracks, Mario reassured the men that they would be safe from harm and the garrison commander was most grateful for this consideration. He then solemnly handed over his own gun personally to Mario instead of stacking it on the pile of arms already surrendered.

The way was now open to the provincial town of Bergamo, situated approximately 40 kilometres south-east of Como and 50 km north-east of Milano.

The town of Bergamo nestled at the foot of the Bergamasco Alps, and in fact comprised two towns. Its population during 1944 was well over 100,000. The old, upper town (Citta Alta) stands on a hillside 400 feet above the lower, more modern part. Its old buildings are surrounded by ruined walls of the old Venetian fortifications together with its ancient fortress. The lower town (Bergamo Bassa), is pleasantly situated around its centre, the Piazza Metteotti. The town has been famous since the 16th century when the Commedia Dell 'Arte originated, with its masked characters, the most famous of which had been Harlequin, the stupid but cunning peasant of the Brembana Valley.

It will be remembered that Manfred and his Partisans had already received word that the Bergamo CLN and Bruno Quarti of the CVL, had taken control of part of the town and had already started to press the Germans into leaving, but the garrison, under SS Unterstürmführer Langen, were undecided what to do. Owing to her knowledge of the German language, Signora Kati Gregis became the secretary of Langen and her work during the negotiations was very useful throughout this difficult period. To avoid any misunderstanding as to the character of Signora Gregis, it is enough to state that she was later arrested and brutally beaten by the Fascists who eventually discovered that she had been collaborating all the time with the Partisans and the CLN.

The insistent demands of Bruno Quarti and CLN assisted by such men as Vittorio Guzzoni, alias Antonio, vice-commandante of the Piazza, Mario Poloni and Antonio Cavelli, known as Maggiore Granata, that the town should be evacuated by the Germans, persuaded Langen to contact Major-General Ebeling, who was responsible for all the German forces in the immediate area, with a request for instructions on what he should do. Groups of local Partisans who had already entered the city were posing an immediate problem, for the slightest incident would be quite sufficient to provoke a full-scale battle. In the Provincial Government Building, one group of Partisans, including the young Dominic

Flessati, eventually took control of one part of the city and had more German prisoners than there were Partisans holding the building. Flessati had gone in with the first, limited force and during one long, tense night, they had rather an anxious time, until at last, Manfred and Invernicci arrived with the main force.

The general situation had not been improved, and was made, in fact, more serious, by the Fascist elements who had barracaded themselves in the nearby houses and were sniping at any Partisan they observed in the streets. The Partisans were, however, able to secure and preserve all public amenities etc: from being destroyed or tampered with. In return, Langen, who had agreed not to attempt to destroy these essential services, had been allowed, together with his troops, to retire to restricted defensive positions in the centre of the city. This position could have remained static for sometime until the eventual arrival of the advancing American forces, but then came the news that a large German Panzer column, in retreat, was fast approaching Bergamo.

Hearing this news, Manfred, together with Invernicci, Mario's courier Renato, and Giuliano Mattioli, borrowed a Fiat car and drove dramatically into the town centre with a large, home-made but imaginative version of the Union Jack, draped over the bonnet. The Fiat roared through the streets, Manfred's intention being to demand immediate unconditional surrender of both German and Fascist forces. However, both these factions opened fire in reply to his demands and the car was forced to withdraw.

Having thus failed, it was obvious that something must be done to stop the Panzer column from reaching Bergamo, as its presence would topple the fine balance and the enemy would undoubtedly take over the city totally. In a convoy of three Fiats, Manfred and his team, together with Invernicci, Renato and a couple of other Partisans, drove from the city heading southwards in the direction of the reported Panzers, then turning off with the hope of joining up with advancing Americans. To take a short-cut, Manfred drove out of the town and across the half deserted German airfield of San Pietro.

Seated with him, Mattioli was suddenly very disturbed when upon looking out of the car window he observed German 88 mm anti-aircraft guns bieng slowly depressed and aimed at them at point-blank range. As the cars drove on the business end of these deadly flak guns slowly followed them across the open, flat landscape.

Understandably alarmed, Mattioli suggested to Manfred that they should turn back and '...get the Hell out of here', but Manfred shrugged off the suggestion, carrying on as if nothing was happening. The guns fortunately remained silent, these Germans too not being certain of the general situation.

Leaving the airfield, to the relief of his companions, the three cars headed south. A short while later, they turned a bend in the road and literally ran slap into the German column. Manfred, in the lead car kept on going, roaring past the column of tanks and vehicles full of troops, but travelling in the opposite direction. Keeping his face forward he only glimpsed the vehicles and lorries as he flashed past, seeing the occasional white blur of German faces looking down on this strange car and its occupants as it raced by. Eventually they came to the end of the column and kept on going, but the last car, some distance behind was cornered. The Germans had eventually realised that the cars were not what they should be, and had managed to block the road, taking the occupants prisoner. These were two Partisans and one of Manfred's NCO wireless-operators.

Driving clear of the immediate danger area, they stopped the cars and attempted to decide what course of action to adopt. It was finally agreed to send Renato off to the nearest village to commandeer another car. Renato was then instructed to drive back to the German column and inform the German Commander that an important telephone call awaited him at the next telephone box along the road. Meanwhile Manfred and Mario drove to the telephone box nearest to them and began ringing through via the operator, to the other boxes ahead of the Germans. A short time later, with great luck, they got through to one at which the German Commander had stopped, following the receipt of Renato's desperate insistence that a call awaited them. Until they actually got through to the German Commander, neither Mario nor Manfred had any real idea what they would say to him, nor how they could stop the column entering Bergamo. When finally Mario heard the German pick up the telephone and heard the German voice at the other end of the line he had to quickly resort to some kind of bluff.

The German picked up the ringing telephone and Mario heard the guttural, 'Ja', from the receiver. Mario spoke quickly and, he hoped, a voice of confidence and authority. Didn't the Commander know that the American 5th Army was in Bergamo, and why were his tanks and vehicles not carrying white flags of surrender. Didn't he realise he was open to immediate attack from both land and air forces by not carrying them?

This sudden statement left the German in complete confusion, but later the column was observed to turn away from Bergamo, escaping northwards by another route.

Meantime, Manfred was already driving south once more where he eventually met the advancing Americans. Making contact with an officer, Manfred was informed that the Americans were not making for the city of Bergamo, and that they could not spare troops, as Manfred requested, to assist him or go to Bergamo to help in the deception of the Germans there. They could let him have, the Americans offered, a couple of armoured cars or something, but Manfred declined. The sight of a few American GI's in the city would be one thing, but a couple of armoured cars might tend to draw too much fire from the enemy and start everyone shooting. Promising to keep in radio contact with Manfred and his Partisans in case any real trouble developed, the Americans moved off towards Como, leaving Manfred to return to Bergamo to discuss the next move in this highly explosive game of chess, and try to continue bluffing the enemy garrison.

On reaching the outskirts of the city, some Fascist women, armed with pistols and rifles, began to open fire on the two Fiats. Manfred slammed on the brakes and was about to retire, when his friend Mattioli stopped him.

'You took me across that airfield with those 88's breathing down our necks without bothering to stop, so we'll go through this trouble spot and you can sweat.' Manfred smiled at his friend and drove on amidst the sniping, bullets whistling all around their car.

During his absence from Bergamo, Major-General Ebeling had himself arrived, and had begun to argue with Unterstürmführer Langen as to what should indeed be done about the situation. Sniping between the Partisans and the German/Fascist troops was slowly increasing. At any moment a full-scale battle might suddenly explode.

In the Partisan Headquarters, situated now in the house of Bruno Quarti, the CVL Leader, Manfred and the others tried to seek an answer to the immediate problem. By nightfall, Manfred decided that they should again try to use bluff on the telephone, so told Quarti to ring through to the Germans, to tell them that the Partisans had now received reinforcements. Quarti made the call, trying to paint as black a picture as he could, outlining the seriousness of the Germans' position.

'The Partisans now have at their disposal,' Quarti warned, 'leading units of the United States Forces who had just arrived in the outskirts of the city, bringing with them guns and armour. Unless,' he continued, 'the two German Commanders decide to surrender themselves together with their men, within two hours, the Partisans and the Americans would be left little choice but to attack and wipe out the German positions. They should therefore, present themselves at the Prefecture within the time given.'

Again there was a tense period of waiting while the Germans mulled over this fresh batch of lies, but this time the trick seemed to work, for the two German Commanders finally decided to surrender. Receiving this news, Manfred sent his terms to the Germans. At 0800 hours, on April 28, 1945, all enemy forces in Bergamo will cease all hostile acts, then surrender all arms to the Partisan Forces.

The Germans discussed this throughout the early hours, sending word at around 4 am that a surrender would take place. A document was drawn up, signed by Langen and sent to the Partisan leaders. This, however, was not accepted; they insisted on a document signed personally by Ebeling.

At about 0700 hours, Ebeling and Langen signed a transcribed document and handed it over at exactly 0800. The German garrison of over 3,000 armed men then formally surrendered themselves, together with their arms and equipment, to the Partisan forces. Bergamo was safe and free at last.

The surrender document sent to Manfred by the German Commanders Ebeling and Langen, read as follows:

To the English Major Manfredi.

To the Bergamo Partisan Command.

I accept the conditions of surrender arranged in discussion on the 27th April, 1945 at 2100 hours.

I confirm that from 8 o'clock onwards there will be no warlike action taken against English, American or Italian patriot detachments. I have given the appropriate order to all the German detachment for which I am responsible.

The surrender of arms has been prepared by me. I assure you

that no deposit of arms has been hidden.

Particulars regarding the handing over of the weapons, the formation of guards for protection, the transport of attached female personnel, etc: have been arranged.

Signed:
EBELING. Major General

Witness:
LANGEN
SS Unterstürmführer.

Just after 0800, the Germans who had been controlling Bergamo and its province for nearly two years, surrendered. Certain elements together with the female personnel mentioned in Ebeling's surrender document, began to leave the town as arranged. As these vehicles began to move off towards the northern frontier, some Fascist officials, fearful of what might happen to them, ran after the trucks, trying desperately to climb aboard, but their late German 'comrades' pushed them off with much violence and insults, leaving them to the mercy of the waiting Partisans.

At this same time, SS Unterstürmführer Langen, who was in fact an Austrian by birth, although aware that his surrender decision had been right for his men, remained true to his SS code, and shortly after the surrender had been negotiated, he withdrew and shot himself. He chose an attempt in the heart, and being left handed, his Luger was pointed sideways as he put pressure on the trigger. Although seriously wounded by the bullet, he lived through this experience.

With the taking of the town, the whole of the surrounding area fell under Partisan control – as far as Alpi Orobie to the north, Lake Iseo to the east, Lake Como to the west and down to Como-Brescia in the south. This allowed the Allied forward troops to completely by-pass Bergamo and reach Como on the 28th April, thereby cutting the last German escape route into Austria. Manfred and his Partisans took charge of 3,000 German troops as well as over 1,000 Italian soldiers following the surrender.

All over Northern Italy the enemy forces were falling back under the Allied advances. A very great contribution was made by the various Partisan groups together with the supporting British missions. On the same date as Bergamo was taken over, Chatillen to the French Border was cleared. Partisans were also closing in on Vicenza, while other bands were in part control of the city of Venice. On the following day, Venice was taken by the Partisans, and Cuneo was liberated by other groups. On this same day, the British 8th Army reached Cuneo while other Allied troops entered the northern capitol of Milan. These successes continued in all areas until early May when the general surrender of the Germans in northern Italy was formally announced. Although a few isolated garrisons continued to resist, these eventually fell to Partisan attacks or were continually harassed until Allied forces reached the areas to take control.

Altogether the achievements of the Partisans in northern Italy were quite impressive. Total casualties known to have been inflicted on the enemy from January to April 1945 was nearly 55,000 killed, wounded or taken prisoner, all but 4,000 of this total being achieved in the crucial month of April. In addition many bridges, trains and motor vehicles, as well as miles of telephone cable and railway track had been cut, destroyed or damaged sufficiently to be completely out of action.

Meanwhile, in Bergamo, Manfred and his men had become the heroes of the hour, the liberators of the city. This was probably the high point of Manfred's life.

Immediately there followed a most exacting time for him and his friend and second in command, Mattioli. The end of the war did not mean the end of their mission or the end of the responsibility to both people and city of Bergamo. First of all Manfred was determined to locate his missing NCO wireless-operator, who had been taken prisoner by the Panzer column. He did not rest in his efforts until the missing man was found, safe and sound, in the jail at Bulzano, where the leader of the Panzer column had deposited him.

Manfred then had the task of organising all the city's immediate requirements, from fuel supplies, food, light etc; to controlling local outbursts of personal or sectarian vendettas. All over Northern Italy, where German forces had surrendered or retreated, there was a period of time before Allied troops arrived to take full control and police action. During this period Partisans or just ordinary village or townspeople dragged out known collaborators or the like, and without too much ceremony, they were stood against a wall and shot. Others were taken and badly beaten by the mob, especially women who had had German lovers.

In his area, Manfred managed to round up most of the suspect collaborators, putting them in jail so as to be out of reach of the would-be lynch-mob. In point of fact his area was one of those with the best records for non-vendetta violence. So successful did he feel his work had been with the Partisans that he requested to remain in Bergamo for several more days to complete his work, this request being granted. One interesting document from this period is a receipt which Manfred kept and which is still in the possession of the family. Written on a slip of paper and given to him by an officer of the first American troops to reach the city, it reads:-

> 672 MED COLL Co.
> A.P.O. 464 U.S. Army.
> Received from S/Ldr Beckett at Bergamo on 1st May 1945 one thousand one hundred and ninety two (1192) prisoner patients (German), and the hospital staff of one hundred and seventy one (171) officers and men.
> (Signed) SAMUEL F DRIVER
> Captain MC
> Commanding 672 Med Coll Co

Manfred's use of the name Beckett is interesting but obscure.

The Partisans were naturally on the crest of a wave. For many this was the end of months, even years, of living by their wits in the forests and mountains, fighting and evading a determined enemy. Manfred and some of his Partisan friends were saluted by the editorial staff of the local newspaper, *Il Giornale Del Popolo*. Manfred and Mario Invernicci, together with other leaders, named as 'Beppi' Laniranchi, Zaverio Fornoni and Giacomo Ruggeri, were thanked publicly for all their hard and gallant work.

Meanwhile, in the local and famous opera house, the Teatro Donizetti, situated in the town centre, almost opposite the Town Hall, the Allied Military Governor, Colonel D. Morley Fletcher, and his staff, arrived and were met by the leading dignataries of the town, headed by the Prefect, Antonio Cavalli, Ezio Zambianchi, the Police Chief and the Secretary General, Dr. Di Pierri. Each were loud in applauding the very real bravery shown by the various Partisan bands and their respective leaders. This event too received front page coverage in the *Il Giornale Del Pofolo*, on May 3, 1945. On the 5th, the paper gave a report, again on the front page, of Manfred's recent activities under the title heading: 'MANFREDI' – *'Un maggiore della RAF fra i 'patrioti'*. Always referred to as Major Manfredi, nowhere at this time does the name Czernin appear, although the town's officials knew his real name.

At some length, the newspaper article explained how popular Manfred had been throughout his two months in the Bergamasco area, being likened to a friend and brother, referred to also as a great fighting companion, brave and audacious. Although it was explained in the fiery yet flowery way the Italians express themselves it was nevertheless exactly how they felt about him. Two days later, Antonio Cavalli and Dr. Di Pierri signed the document which conferred on Manfred the title of Honorary Citizen of the Town of Bergamo, the first 'foreigner' so honoured.

By now the town was in the hands of the Allies, the 1st United States Armoured Division having been the first to arrive on April 29. During June victory celebrations took place, the various Partisan bands marching proudly through the city centre to parade in the piazza in front of the Town Hall. Leading his particular band along streets lined with the citizens of this provincial capital he wore his battledress, his stout mountain boots and his ski-cap with its large peak. It rained slightly on and off during the parade but this did not in any way dampen the festivities. Manfred carried a small bunch of flowers that had been pressed into his hand. Marching with him were the Partisan patriots. 'The rebels of yesterday, men of law and order today, the builders of tomorrow.'

At long last the war even felt over, it was finished. The cheering, happy and grateful people of Bergamo brought Manfred's war to a wonderful and fitting climax.

CHAPTER TEN

The Last Years

Major Raoul Lufbery, the famous French/American fighter pilot, who flew with the Lafayette Escadrille during World War One, once said, 'There will be no after the war for a fighter pilot.' Lufbery himself did not live to see the end of that war to prove his theory, for he was killed in 1918. While Manfred had been an SOE agent as well as a fighter pilot in the Second World War, this somewhat profound statement may well have applied to him.

Immediately after the war, Manfred was still riding high upon his own personal successes. Compared with many soldiers, sailors or airmen, his had been a successful war in many ways. Soon after the German surrender, a very grateful Bergamo conferred on him, as mentioned in the previous chapter, the title of '*Cittadinanza Onoraria*'. For his second, highly successful mission behind the enemy lines, the British conferred on him the award of the Distinguished Service Order.

Relieved of his duties at last, Manfred went south to Ravello for a short stay and for a well-earned rest. On his instigation, as already related, men of No 1 Special Force spent many restful hours at the 'Swallow's Nest' and continued to do so immediately after the end of hostilities in Italy. During this particular rest period a friend of Manfred's, who also knew his mother, stayed there too and wrote at this time to Mrs Frost about the beauty of Ravello, as he sat one evening with Manfred.

> It is too utterly lovely here. At the moment Manfred is playing the piano, the light on the fishing boats down below are coming out one by one, like reflections of the stars above them, and there is such an atmosphere of peace as I've not felt for years.

The last time Manfred went to be dropped in the North he looked very tired, but he has done a remarkably fine piece of work and everyone is immensely proud of him. Now he has been living in the sun and sea for a week and looks splendidly (well). He does so love this place.

We speak continuously of his daughter and small son, and I've seen all the snaps of them. He is so very proud of them.

One can easily picture the peace and beauty of Ravello from these brief extracts, and also how people in Italy felt about him.

During a visit to Rome shortly after this, he took the opportunity of seeing his friend Monsignor Hugh O'Flaherty, the famous Irish priest who had done such courageous and dangerous work during the war, helping Allied prisoners of war who had escaped captivity or political refugees to get away from the Germans, via the Vatican. Hugh O'Flaherty asked Manfred if he would like to be presented to the Pope; Manfred indicated that he would. So it was that Manfred stood with some twenty or so people during the next audience held by Pope Pius XII.

They all stood in a long line while the Pope slowly walked along from person to person, saying a few words to each one. Finally he came to Manfred and was introduced. They spoke for a few moments about Manfred's duties during the war and what he had achieved in the North. Then the Pope asked,

'Are you a Catholic, Czernin?'

'No your Holiness, I am an atheist,' he replied.

The Pope smiled, nodded, and then moved to the next person, but then he half-turned and looking back at Manfred said,

'Not a very clever thing to be.'

Manfred was released from the ranks of Special Forces on August 1, 1945, having returned to England where he was sent to Fighter Command Headquarters at Bentley Priory. It was as well he had left Italy when he did for he managed to put up a 'black' during a poker game in Naples. He had always been an ardent card player, excelling at poker, bridge and chemin-de-fer. This sort of thing was bound to happen to a person like Manfred who could be so well liked by some people and be disliked by others. His old wartime comrade Hedley Vincent could not stand him because he was such a romancer and made stories up all the time. This had always been true but all his tales were so easy to check and confirm or dismiss that they could only have been said or told to see how others would react to them.

Strangely enough, Manfred now had so many real and true adventures one would imagine that he had little reason for making up others, but he continued to do so. Provided one knew him, allowances could be made, but to others they must have seemed completely true. Even the sobering effect of war did not change his storytelling. On his first mission he had once told Tom Rowarth, who had been in the Carnia region with him, that he had been married several times and that his first wife had been killed in a car accident on their honeymoon!

Peter Townsend, who had been his commanding officer briefly in 1940, remembers hearing one story that happened during the Battle of Britain, no doubt started by Manfred himself. A German airman was supposed to have been brought down at Biggin Hill, and Manfred was escorting him when the German kicked and insulted the body of a dead British airman. Manfred, so the story goes, gave the German a piece of his mind and then shot him in the stomach. This story is similar to the one already mentioned when Manfred told a friend that he had had to shoot one of his band because, although warned repeatedly, this one Partisan shot down an unarmed German prisoner. Oddly enough the parallels are completely opposite in this story.

Even Richard Hewitt, the Commander of No 1 Special Force thought Manfred to be a complete 'Bull-shitter' and a ghastly romancer, but for all that one could not help but like and admire him as a man. The one thing on which everyone agreed was that whatever Manfred might lack in his make-up, it was not courage. Richard Hewitt recalls that it was not just a case of being brave, many men were brave, but Manfred was really a man who just had no fear whatsoever; he '... was utterly fearless.' As already related his comrade during 1940, Harold Bird-Wilson, thought him the '... bravest man I ever knew.'

Perhaps no one can know what exactly made Manfred tick, but perhaps no one person can ever know everything about any human being. In 1940 some members of his own family thought the stories about his exploits in the RAF were just more typical romantic tales, until he was decorated, and then later in the war, other decorations came!

His good looks too had not helped in some ways. Women were completely captivated by him, his handsome features, his seemingly honest charm, his knowing ways, and his glamorous background. He rarely had any trouble in, what one would describe today as 'pulling the birds.' In many ways he lived hard and played hard.

After a short stay at Bentley Priory and some leave to see again his family, Manfred was sent to 11 Group's Central Flying Establishment based at RAF Tangmere, his old stamping ground of August 1940 and the scene on his 'Line Shooter's Medal'. How long ago that now seemed.

Following a check-out by an instructor, Manfred again became the pilot, adding some 63 flying hours on various types of aeroplanes between August and September 1945. Unfortunately his log-book, which he had not used since 1943, does not record the types he flew during this period.

In these months he had been living at Athenaeum Court, Piccadilly in a Service flat, but difficulties had arisen between Manfred and Maud. The war years had changed and affected their lives considerably and then Manfred, who had only been offered a ground job in the Royal Air Force, decided to leave the Service and resign his commission. This he did and was officially released from the RAF on September 27, his last day of service being listed as January 4, 1946.

One incident worthy of mention happened while Manfred was still in uniform. He was having a drink in a bar one evening with some friends when he heard a man across the room, say with a voice slightly raised for all to hear.

'Look at that fellow over there with the DSO, MC and DFC, how can he possibly have them all?' True it was unusual to have a combination of these three decorations, but the man was wrong. Manfred quietly put down his glass, crossed the room and hit the man squarely on the jaw, sending him crashing to the floor. Manfred, his honour duly satisfied, returned to the bar, his drink and his friends.

Leaving the RAF, Manfred was without a job, without any sort of trade or profession, and the immediate question was What to do now? Up to this time his Service pay, supplemented fairly regularly with financial help from his mother, enabled Maud and him to live reasonably well. Maud's mother and father, but particularly her mother, had still not forgiven her for marrying Manfred in 1939 and had refused to see either her or the two children, and it was understood that they would remain oblivious of them unless Maud and Manfred divorced.

Everything now had come to a head. He was without a job but Maud had the offer of financial help from her parents if she divorced Manfred. Mrs. Frost did try to reason with the Hamiltons hoping to revive their previous friendly associations that had existed between them years earlier, but Mrs Hamilton was adamant. In due course Maud and Manfred, already lost to each other in many ways during the war, were divorced. In 1941, Mrs Frost had purchased a cottage at Lamberhurst in Kent, where now the family lived until 1956.

Yet although divorced, Manfred and Maud were not totally without love for one another. They remained in close friendship throughout the rest of his life and although other women continually came into his life there was always a strong bond between them. Had he not died when he did they may even have re-married. Not that Maud did not have her men friends too, but Manfred was really the only man she ever loved. A very real affection for one another remained right up till the end.

Early in 1947 Manfred, together with an old Air Force friend, R. B. Pakenham, and this friend's girlfriend (whom Manfred eventually won over!), decided to try to set up an air freight and transport business in Johannesburg. They scraped together, just enough cash to purchase a twin-engined Avro Anson (G-AJHK) in early May 1947 and following much preparation they were finally ready to go on the 11th. If nothing else, it was a most pleasant trip to South Africa, and they took the opportunity to see some of the world en route.

From Gatwick Airport they flew across to France landing at Marseille via Toussus-le-Noble. Then on the 14th they flew to Naples via the Italian capital of Rome. Two days later they flew across to Brindisi, a place which brought back vivid memories to Manfred and his time with Special Forces. From Brindisi they flew across to the Greek capital of Athens. Following a most pleasant two day stay over in Athens, they flew down to the island of Crete before going on to Cairo. Luxor-Wadi, Haifa-Khartoum-Malakal-Juba, followed, then on to Kisumu, arriving at Nairobi on the 26th. Taking off again on the 29th they were forced to turn back when engine trouble developed, which delayed them until June 5 but eventually they reached Johannesburg via Lusaka, Salisbury and Bulawayo. The journey ended on June 10, Manfred and Pakenham having flown the whole journey in 66 hours 10 minutes flying time.

After their arrival they began to plan the business end of their project but soon came to realize that the expenses in setting it all up, airfield taxes, equipment, staff, advertising, insurances, etc: was going to be far above their expectation and financially too much for them so reluctantly the idea had to be dropped.

Manfred was then employed by a firm of stockbrokers, Dalrymple and Franks (no relation to the author) in Johannesburg, and he remained with them until January 1949.

In the late summer of 1948, Manfred became very ill, although he told nobody of his problem, exactly as he had told no-one of his illness in 1934. Then he contracted pneumonia and was taken off to a nearby hospital. As he began to recover from this, he complained to his doctors of having severe pains in his hip. The area was X-rayed and it was diagnosed to be cancer of the hip joint. This of course meant surgery but as yet he was not strong enough to undergo an operation. While regaining his strength he was visited by a friend and Manfred told him of the new complication. This friend told him that he knew a faith healer whom he felt sure could help him. Manfred laughed at the idea, saying that he didn't believe in faith healers. This man, said his friend, did not mind if he believed or not, so Manfred's objections to seeing him were brushed aside and he agreed, although somewhat reluctantly, to have the man see him.

The faith healer, or 'magnetic-healer' as he preferred to call himself, visited Manfred on two occasions. Then, shortly before the operation was due, another X-ray was taken. The result showed a fantastic improvement, so much so that the doctors found it difficult to believe the evidence before them. In October he had been hobbling about on sticks, yet by November, Manfred was walking about quite happily and looking much more like his old self again. It seemed a miracle, but he was completely cured.

Following this period of hospitalization he was offered, what appeared to be, a plum job, commanding a high salary, and with very considerable prospects. This new position commenced on January 1, 1949, his new employers sending him, with two other company men, to Rome. Manfred with his knowledge of Italy and speaking the language fluently, acted as both guide and interpreter.

Everything appeared to go smoothly, the two associates mal successful business transactions and contracts, which was the wh object of the trip. In February, when Manfred's mother visited him in Rome, everything was still proceeding perfectly well but then suddenly his two companions just disappeared, taking with them all the cash they had collected. Manfred was left high and dry and was soon out of a job yet again.

For a while he stayed at the Grand Hotel in Rome, hoping to find work while supplementing his income at the card tables at the local night clubs, but then in April disaster struck. Manfred, while gambling at a club got in too deep and borrowed a large sum of money from a friend then proceeded to lose this too. His mother said she would cover the loss but at the time it was absolutely forbidden to send money out from England. Fortunately a friend of hers, an Italian who had settled in England, acted as a go-between. She settled the debt and gave Manfred enough money to last just one month, after which, she told him, he must find a job, stop gambling and fend for himself.

After this episode, Mrs Frost heard nothing from him for over a year. Eventually he turned up in Paris where he had acquired a position with the Rootes Car Company, whose offices were in the Champs Elysées. Out of the blue he suddenly wrote to her at Hexworthy in Devon where she was residing, asking her to come over to Paris for a visit, which of course she was only too happy to do.

Later she learned of yet another serious period of illness that Manfred had gone through. He had suffered terribly from stomach ulcers ever since his months with the Partisans and his condition had gradually worsened, giving him much pain. After a thorough examination his Paris doctor told him that he must have part of his stomach removed and it came at a time when he received news from England that his mother was dying in Plymouth. She of course, while seriously ill, knew nothing of her son's condition. Maud sent a telegraph to him and he immediately replied that he would try to visit England. Then fortunately she began to recover and was taken off the danger list, so Manfred remained in Paris undergoing his own operation in July. His doctors told him that he must stay in hospital for at least six weeks afterwards, but typically, he was holidaymaking in Majorca three weeks later and was back at work in October. It was then he wrote to his mother, she too now fully recovered. His letter was dated October 14, 1953.

Darling Mama,

I'm very glad to hear you are feeling much better, and I will tell you the full story of my operation. I was having severe pains all through April and May and had an X-ray which showed that my ulcers were definitely not only in a bad way but becoming cancerous. It was decided that my stomach had to be removed. Fortunately I had a wonderful surgeon and although the operation lasted five hours, I came through this in an incredibly short space of time; so much so that even the surgeon was amazed. I am completely fit and can eat and drink everything, and thank God, for the first time in eight years, I am completely free from pain.

I did not want to worry you with this news, and it is also the reason that I could not come over to see you at once as I was considered unfit to travel. Twice I rang up the hospital for news of you but the damned hospital was too mean to send me word how you were.

Here I am getting on fine and am now in charge of the sales and what will be great fun, on the 22nd I am going to Rome for ten days to represent Rootes at an extremely important conference. I hear that you may be coming to Italy about that time too, so I am giving you my address in Rome which is: Hotel Boston, Via Lombardia, Rome, where I shall be staying till the 31st. Maybe we may meet there, in any case I shall be coming to Lamberhurst for Christmas and I am looking forward to seeing you. By the way, you never get my address quite right and you will see what it is from the heading.

All my love,
Manfred

P.S. I saw Maud who came over for the weekend and was in very good form and told me all your news.

In spite of professing to be an atheist, it is interesting to see that he thanks his God for being free from pain.

Following this business trip to Rome, he returned to England, again out of a job, for the French government had suddenly decided that companies based in France should not employ labour from other countries and so he had to leave.

He was however, soon re-employed, again in the car industry, this time in the London office of the Renault Group. The job entailed much travelling up and down the country, to and from the Midlands. On one of these trips, going to Wolverhampton, he crashed badly in his car (he invariably drove too fast), putting himself in hospital in Burton-on-Trent. Coming out of hospital he went straight to Maud, staying with her to convalesce for almost three months.

He had a period of car smashes at about this time, all due to his love of fast cars and excessive speed. Manfred even put one of his close friends flat on his back with a slipped disc, through a motoring accident. This friend was Walter Parslow who worked for another car firm in Wolverhampton. They would often meet, Manfred staying with him at Walter's beautiful cottage near Stafford, with its picturesque garden and bubbling fountain pool. Both being ex-servicemen and both being in the same line of business, they had a great deal in common. Walter Parslow remembers Manfred as a man who worked hard and played hard, with a great liking for whisky, which was his favourite drink.

Again in England, Manfred saw more of Maud and suddenly all the past years slipped away and while there was no firm reconciliation between them they enjoyed each other's company again. To some extent Manfred began to settle a little at this time. He often stayed with Maud and the children, usually trying to dine with them at least once a week. He never missed a family birthday and ensured that each Christmas they were together. He did not, however, settle down from his gambling and continued to enjoy all forms of night life. On occasions he was extremely lucky, once picking up over £2,000 during one card session. For a few days he would live it up but when the winnings dwindled he would be at the tables again.

Manfred's health was never the same after his operation in Paris and in fact soon after his return to England had to undergo further surgery. Luck and ill health seemed all against him during the mid-1950s. In 1955 his brother Paul, who had lost his left leg in the shooting incident in 1921 and had suffered from the injury ever since, died in his sleep at his home in Austria. He left a wife and four children.

For all his adversities, Manfred was still very much the man about town, well liked by his few really close friends, but his somewhat 'here today, gone tomorrow' attitude to everyday life made him rather detached in these years. His unreliability and uncertain attitude made it difficult to make lasting ties with anyone. He still possessed that indefinable charm which endeared him to everyone he met and he was still extremely attractive to the opposite sex. Unfortunately although his charm did endear him to nearly everyone he met and knew, he was rarely taken too seriously and he could never escape from the air of unreliability. He would break appointments without thinking too much about it and yet on other occasions he could give the impression that if it became necessary he would give his life for a friend without a second thought. No one could ever tell just how much he really cared for people but of his children he was very fond and very proud. Like any proud father he carried photographs of Carolyn and Nicholas in his wallet and enjoyed showing them to his friends on every opportunity.

Being in London again, he was able, during the summer months to awake his passion for cricket. Still a member of the MCC he spent many Saturday afternoons at Lords. It was here one afternoon that he ran into Hugh Latimer with whom he had been at Oundle School. Even after all those years, Latimer, now a famous actor, remembers Manfred greeting him like a long-lost brother. Latimer also recalls clearly Manfred's deep voice which was nevertheless very soft and gentle and which matched so much his charming ways.

Another friend was Pat Ricard and his wife, who both remember Manfred as something of a philosopher. Pat and Manfred would often meet at Lords on a Saturday and would return to Pat's W2 mews house, spending the warm summer evenings talking over drinks, or perhaps they would all go out for a meal.

Manfred's skill at unarmed combat, which had remained with him since his SOE days in Italy, came in useful one dark evening when he was returning to his own flat. Crossing Belgrave Square one night he sensed that two men who were following him were up to no good. Whether they were out for a bit of fun or intended to rob him he never discovered, but they soon found to their cost that to attack this tall, slightly balding man was a mistake. As the first man pounced, one swift blow and a twist of his body sent his opponent over Manfred's back and crashing to the ground. The second man hesitated then turned and ran, followed rapidly by the first who was still wondering what had happened in the first place.

In 1957, his employers sent him to Milan on business where he was to be met by one of the company's agents. Travelling by train, they stopped at Domodossola to check the passengers through customs. On checking through their list of doubtful persons, the customs officials found the name of Count Manfred Czernin as being part of a company that had become fraudulently bankrupt. He was immediately arrested and ended up in the gaol in Florence.

It was a bad time to be imprisoned in Italy, some people having been known to disappear for months while police investigations went on. Manfred managed to get an Italian to take a message out for him, addressed to his old wartime associate Tom Rowarth, who lived in Milan. Rowarth immediately engaged his own lawyer, who in due course, discovered that somehow Manfred had been made an honorary president of a company at the end of the war and it had subsequently become bankrupt; hence Manfred's name appeared on a list of undesirables. As it was he remained in prison for some four months before the lawyer was able to clear his name and his association, then get him released from custody. On gaining his freedom, Manfred, too, managed to smuggle out of the prison a letter from a cell-mate who had been locked away for several weeks without any form of contact with his family or friends, or even having had a trial. Following this episode, Manfred spent some time with friends in Rome.

In 1958 Manfred was interviewed for a post of sales manager with Fiat Limited, in England. The interview was conducted by Mr G. Boella, director of the company in England. Mr Boella was impressed with Manfred's strong personality and his Italian background and knowledge, which secured for him the post which he commenced on September 22.

Manfred was with Fiats for the last four years of his life. For him, following the trials and tribulations of the post-war years, it was to be four happy years, for at last he was doing a job he really liked and one that was worth his mettle. Again his dynamic character was allowed to flourish. He was liked by everyone and soon became known as a very live wire within the car industry, his previous experience standing him in good stead. Although life had now taken on a new meaning for him he was again now, rarely free from pain. He continued to try and hide it but his stomach area continued to give him much trouble. He had always been a heavy drinker, but now, without any real digestive system, the alcohol he drank went almost directly into the bloodstream giving the impression to those who did not know him, that he drank too much and was easily intoxicated. Alcohol did, however, give him some freedom from his pain, but as always he refused to admit that he was even slightly unwell or uncomfortable. He was always the fighter.

From two small, almost insignificant, items from his private life we have some indication of his changing attitude to life and people. He lived in a flat in Chatworth Court, in Pembroke Road, near Earl's Court, and one day he confided to his mother:

'When I shut my front door and know no one can disturb me, I feel happy.' Strange words for someone who was normally very sociable and had always enjoyed other people's company.

The second item refers to a clock that he had in his flat, which he fixed to run backwards. When a friend asked why he kept it Manfred remarked:

'When I look at it, it reminds me that time itself is not important, only what one does with time.'

Once alone in his flat and with his thoughts he would often sit quietly thinking over his past life and occasionally reading. His favourite book, which he read many times, was Tolkien's *Lord of the Rings*.

His daughter Carolyn had now grown into a beautiful young woman, Manfred beginning to take her out to dine once or twice a month to show her off to his friends with very real pride.

While with Fiats he represented them on the Council of all Foreign Car Manufacturers and he was also to be seen at the Annual Motor Show in London. In fact at one of these shows a man said to him:

'You are working for Fiats aren't you?' Another man who was standing close by, overheard this question, and turned and replied.

'Czernin doesn't work for Fiats, he is Fiats.' Not true of course, but the compliment does show how well he was thought of in the industry.

While with Fiats he again went down with pneumonia. His doctor sent him to bed immediately, but the following day he was back at his desk, result – he went down with double pneumonia. This was the obstinacy in his character and we have another insight into this part of his personality. He met again his old wartime friend Hiram Smith, now a Wing Commander, and who had remained in the Royal Air Force after the war, having spent the immediate post war years in Germany and in Pakistan. One evening Hiram and his wife dined out with Manfred at the La Rascasse Club and Manfred ordered

Schnitzel. In attempting a light sprinkling of paprika over it the top came off the container, depositing a heavy covering, about a quarter of an inch thick, all over his food. Most people would have returned it to the kitchen, apologised, and requested another serving but not Manfred, who foolishly or not, was determined not to be beaten by this surfeit of paprika no matter how difficult it made the meal to swallow.

In 1960 he visited his father, Otto Czernin, who lived in the beautiful town of Salzburg in Austria. After all the years apart, the mutual love of music suddenly drew them very close together. At last the rift between them was healed and Otto saw in Manfred his own double. Although his father's sight was beginning to fail in these his last years, he played the violin to a most appreciative son. Otto had in fact been an accomplished violinist since his youth. His teacher in Vienna in the 1890s had told Otto's mother that he should use his obvious talent and become a professional violinist instead of entering the diplomatic service. Not unnaturally, in the 1890s this was not considered a suitable career for a Count, his family refusing to entertain such a career, but he never gave it up and always played most beautifully all his life. Manfred, although very fond of good music never really mastered any musical instrument properly, although he had played the violin at school and loved to improvise on the piano.

During the early summer of 1962, Manfred was busily planning Fiats' Sales Programme for the following year. Mr Boella had been checking through the propositions put before him and casually remarked that he hoped all would be well for the 1963 programme. Manfred smiled and looked up saying:

'We shall never go back. We will go up and up and up.' He was to be proven correct in his belief, but never lived to see how true his prediction turned out.

In the spring came word of the Special Forces Reunion which was to be held in Brussels. Manfred wanted very much to attend but his finances were low. Carolyn, who had just had her 21st birthday, gave some of her birthday money to her father, insisting he should go and meet his old comrades. With grateful thanks he agreed and she arranged for his trip. Flying to the Belgian capital at the end of May he attended the Reunion and enjoyed himself very much. As for Carolyn, it was to prove one of the last times she was able to come anywhere near thanking him for all he had done for her.

Shortly after his return from Brussels came the news of the passing in Salzburg of his father. It was June and the weather was warm and fine, but for Manfred it was a time for some sadness. His life too was nearing its end, its course nearly run. That year at the Motor Show, he ran into his old friend Richard Ayling, with whom he had first learned to fly back in 1935. They had a pleasant chat about old times, taking a few drinks at the bar. To Ayling, Manfred seemed as always so full of life and not a bit like a man so close to death.

The first touch of autumn came to London as September gave way to October. Manfred visited his mother on the Wednesday evening of that first October week. As the sky darkened they sat in silence listening to records of Vivaldi, Albinoni and other early Italian composers, on the gramaphone. He had never lost his love of good music. It was a nostalgic evening and the last they were to share together, happily they were alone with each other, the grey haired lady and her son.

Manfred, this same day, had, for the first time in his life visited a fortune teller. She told him everything about his past, his war years, the family, Cimbrone, his job – in fact everything there was to know about his past. He was so impressed that he telephoned Maud as soon as he returned home and she made an appointment to go and see the woman the next day. They had both made their appointments under assumed names but as soon as Maud walked in the fortune teller said:

'I saw your ex-husband yesterday. You have always been very close, but the ties will be snapped at the end of the week.'

On the Friday, Manfred returned from his office, having arranged to take a lady friend and her daughter out for the evening. Maud telephoned him to ask if he would make a fourth for bridge but he declined, having already planned his evening out. Manfred and his two guests went to a West-End night-club and after a meal and a floor show, Manfred sat playing chemin-de-fer at the card tables. They returned to his flat around midnight where after a nightcap he took a single sleeping pill, washed it down with a can of apple-juice from the refrigerator and then went to bed.

Manfred Czernin, full of life and adventure, brave and fearless warrior, man of action, died peacefully in his sleep following a heart attack during the early hours of Saturday October 6, 1962. His poor body had finally succumbed to the alcohol he used to fight his pain.

Manfred's mortal ashes were buried at Ravello by courtesy of a friend of Mrs Frost who had purchased the beautiful villa Cimbrone. Here he rests from his earthly labours in the warm Italian sun, in the land of his childhood, the country he loved.

Epilogue

The Times Wednesday October 17, 1962.

Count Manfred Czernin.

Group Captain H. Bird-Wilson, CBE, DSO, DFC, AFC, writes:-

'It would be wrong to allow a person of the calibre of Squadron Leader Manfred B. Czernin DSO MC DFC to depart from this life without paying tribute to the magnificent service that he, an Austrian, so willingly gave his adopted country during the Second World War. Czernin's RAF service record must be unique, because he not only served with the utmost gallantry in the RAF but was seconded to Special Forces in the latter part of the war and was dropped twice behind enemy lines in Northern Italy.

'I served with Czernin in 17 Squadron in France and throughout the Battle of Britain. He will always be remembered by his fellow pilots for his keenness to engage the enemy and for his disregard of personal risk in carrying out head-on attacks on large formations of enemy aircraft in his Hurricane. When awarded the DFC in August 1940, he was credited with the destruction of nine German aircraft. Later he commanded his own Spitfire squadron.

'In June 1944, Czernin was dropped into enemy occupied territory and regardless of his own safety and through a courageous action greatly contributed to the success of the major plan. For this he received the MC.

'In March 1945, he was parachuted again into Northern Italy and was given the task of coordinating various scattered partisan units into a unified command. Due to his personal courage, aggressiveness and high qualities of leadership the force of partisans under his direction subdued a number of outlying garrisons and eventually secured the unconditional surrender of Bergamo from the German

General. With the partisan leader he drove into Bergamo in a cab draped with the Union Jack. For this notable contribution to the Allied success in Northern Italy he received the DSO.

'I have never known a braver officer.'

* * *

At Manfred's funeral, among all the flowers and wreaths outside the Chapel, was one small bunch of violets. His son and daughter looked at the small card attached. It read: 'Manfredi Addio. The Fiammi Verdi.'

* * *

October 26, 1962

Gentile Signora,

The news contained in your kind letter of October 17 caused me great sadness,inasmuch as I was linked to my friend Manfredi by sincere fraternal affection. We have spent both happy and tragic moments together, during the duration in the mountains and during the negotiations for surrender in various localities, as far as Bergamo. This, my own city has awarded its honorary citizenship to Manfredi for his outstanding merits.

Last August during a quick trip to Ravello with my wife and in the course of a brief visit to the gardens of Villa Cimbrone, I remembered Manfredi, lively and dynamic, when he was showing us with pride the photographs of his delightful children. It is very sad to think how you will return there.

If I had known the day your son's ashes arrived at Ravello, I would, of course, brought my own floral tribute and offered you my own expressions of heartfelt grief.

Dear Signora, in the event of your making a journey to Milan I would wish to see you in person, but even more I wish to greet you tenderly and to confirm to you the friendship that I entertain for my friend Manfredi.

Believe me,
Mario Invernicci.

* * *

November 16, 1962

MUNICIPALITY OF BERGAMO

This Municipality has learned with great grief the news of the death of your beloved son Count Manfred Czernin.

The illustrious deceased co-operated heroically and well with the Patriots of Bergamo in the struggle for National Liberty and for the salvation of this city from the onslaughts of war. A grateful Bergamo conferred on him in 1945 the 'Honorary Citizenship of the City'. Distinguished Signora, have the goodness to accept, in the name of the Civic Administration and the whole populace, the sincere expression of our most heartfelt condolences.

With great esteem and respectful wishes.

* * *

Manfredi, addio

APPENDIX A

RECORD OF SERVICE

Appointments and Promotions

Short Service Commission as Acting Pilot Officer on probation, General Duties Branch RAF.	16 April 1935
Graded as Pilot Officer on probation	16 April 1936
Transferred to Reserve Class A	16 August 1937
Confirmed in appointment	30 June 1938
Flying Officer	28 March 1940
Flight Lieutenant (Acting)	19 March 1941
War Substantive Flight Lieutenant	28 March 1941
Squadron Leader (Acting)	17 December 1941
Relinquished Acting Squadron Leader	20 January 1942
Temporary Squadron Leader	1 June 1942
Released	2 October 1945
Last day of Service	4 January 1946

Movements

RAF Depot Inland Area, Uxbridge, Middx.	16 April 1935
6 Flying Training School, Netheravon, Wilts.	7 May 1935
57(B) Squadron ADGB, Upper Heyford, Oxon.	24 February 1936
RAF Depot, Uxbridge.	10 March 1936
Depot Training Command, Uxbridge.	21 June 1936
83(B) Squadron, West Freugh, Scotland.	5 December 1936
RAFO, ERFTS, Hanworth.	20 June 1938
RAFO, ERFTS, Hanworth.	14 August 1939
No 4 AOS, West Freugh.	2 September 1939
No 1 AOS, Pembrey.	12 September 1939

Record of Services cont:

No 1 Ferry Pilots Pool, Hucknall, Notts.	20 September 1939
No 12 Group Pool, Aston Down, Glos.	10 December 1939
504 Squadron, Debden, Essex.	23 January 1940
213 Squadron, Wittering, Northants.	6 February 1940
85 Squadron, BEF, France.	9 May 1940
17 Squadron, Martlesham, Suffolk & France.	8 June 1940
17 Squadron, Debden, Martlesham, Tangmere, Martlesham	19 June 1940
52 Operational Training Unit, Debden.	31 May 1941
65 Squadron, Tangmere.	15 December 1941
222 Squadron, North Weald, Essex.	21 December 1941
41 Squadron, West Hamptnett, Sussex.	20 January 1942
RAF Tangmere.	15 February 1942
301 Maintenance Unit, India.	28 February 1942
146 Squadron, India & Assam.	16 March 1942
224 Group, India.	18 November 1942
BHQ Bombay, India.	17 April 1943
28 Group, Uxbridge.	7 May 1943
Air Ministry Unit, London. (for duty in AI 10)	28 September 1943
HQ Fighter Command, Bentley Priory, Middx.	1 August 1945
Central Flying Establishment, Tangmere.	12 August 1945
100 Personnel Despatch Centre (for release)	27 September 1945

APPENDIX B

The following two lists show Manfred's personal combat claims.
The first list is taken directly from his flying log-book together with his comments and his own running total of victories.
List two is the list of his victories in the light of present day research and knowledge, giving also the German units where known.

Flying Officer Manfred Czernin's victories and notes taken from his Flying-log Book.

Four victories carried forward from Log Book No 3, lost in France, May 1940.

Date	*Remarks*	*Tally*
June 12	Patrol St Valerie. Saw 4 He111Ks shot all down. My own confirmed.	Fifth confirmed.
June 14	Patrol Seine. 5 Me109s. Got one unconfirmed.	
July 12	Convoy Patrol. Saw 3 Do17s. Got one unconfirmed.	
July 24	X Raid. Shot up one Ju88 but it did not crash.	
August 18	X Raid. Ran into about 200 EA. Got one possible Me109.	
August 21	Leading Red Section. Section attacked and destroyed one Ju88.	Fifth 1/3 confirmed.

August 25	Interception of big raid. Got 3 Me110s confirmed.	Sixth, seventh & eighth 1/3 confirmed.
September 3	X Raid. Ran into 150-200 EA. Got 2 Me110s confirmed myself.	Ninth & tenth 1/3 confirmed.
September 5	X Raid. Ran into 15 He111s & 30 Me109s. Bagged one Me109 confirmed, & shared one He111 confirmed with Sgt Chew & got one probable He111.	Eleventh 5/6 confirmed.
September 11	X Raid. Ran into about 15 Me110s. Bagged one Me110 confirmed.	Twelfth 5/6 confirmed. Got awarded DFC.
September 19	X Raid. Section attacked & destroyed one Ju88. Leading Red section.	Thirteenth 1/6 confirmed
September 24	X Raid. Ran into some Me109s. Got one probable.	
September 27	X Raid. Ran into Me110s. Got one confirmed.	Fourteenth 1/6 confirmed.
October 14	Intercepted & damaged 1 Do17 in 10/10th cloud.	
October 24	X Raid. Section intercepted & destroyed 1 Do17.	Fourteenth ½ confirmed.
October 28	Intercepted one Do215 and damaged it severely.	
October 28	Scramble over base. Damaged 1 Do215.	
October 30	X Raid. Got 1 Me109 confirmed.	Fifteenth ½ confirmed.
November 17	Attacked formation of bombers. Wops. Got caught napping & was myself shot down. Baled out OK.	

Flying Officer Count M B Czernin's combat victories during 1940.

Date	*Type*	*Result*	*Remarks*
May 19	Heinkel 111 K	*Destroyed*	During Battle of France
May 19	Heinkel 111 K	Unconfirmed	During Battle of France
May 19	Dornier 17 Z	*Destroyed*	During Battle of France
May 19	Dornier 17 Z	*Destroyed*	During Battle of France
May 20	Henschel 126	*Destroyed*	During Battle of France
Jun 12	Heinkel 111 K	*Destroyed*	During Battle of France off Le Havre
Jun 14	Messerschmitt bf 109E	Unconfirmed	During Battle of France Seine Estuary
Jul 12	Dornier 17 Z	*Destroyed*	From II/KG2. Crashed into sea
Jul 24	Junkers 88 A-1	Damaged	
Aug 8	Junkers 88 A-1	Damaged	East of Aldeburgh
Aug 18	Messerschmitt bf 109E	Damaged	Chased Ea to French Coast
Aug 21	Junkers 88 A-1	*Destroyed*	Shared with SL Williams and Sgt Bartlett. From II/KG54. Crashed into sea off I of W.
Aug 25	Messerschmitt bf 110 C-4	*Destroyed*	From I/ZG2 Crashed into sea off Portland.
Aug 25	Messerschmitt bf 110 C-4	*Destroyed*	From I/ZG2 Crashed into sea off Portland.
Aug 25	Messerschmitt bf 110 C-4	*Destroyed*	Shared with 609 Squadron. Crashed near Warmwell.
Sep 3	Messerschmitt bf 110 C-4	*Destroyed*	From I/ZG2
Sep 3	Messerschmitt bf 110 C-4	*Destroyed*	Either from I/ZG2 (also claimed by 46 Sdn) or from 6/ZG26 which crashed in France.
Sep 5	Heinkel 111 H-3	*Destroyed*	From 7/KG53. This Heinkel was however, finished off by Lock of 41 Sqdn. Coded A1+CR
Sep 5	Heinkel 111 H-3	*Destroyed*	From 7/KG53. Shared with Sgt Chew. Crashed near Chatham. Coded A1+GR
Sep 5	Messerschmitt bf 109E	*Destroyed*	From 9/JG54. Crashed at South Benfleet.
Sep 11	Messerschmitt bf 110 C-4	*Destroyed*	From Stab II/ZG26. Crashed into the sea. Coded 3U+HM
Sep 19	Junkers 88 A-1	*Destroyed*	From I/KGr806. Crashed in sea. Shared with Sgts Bartlett & Griffiths.
Sep 24	Messerschmitt bf 109E	Probable	Off Margate. No German losses
Sep 27	Messerschmitt bf 110 D-3	*Destroyed*	From V/LG1
Oct 14	Dornier 17 Z-2	Damaged	From I/NJG2. Shared with PO Pittman. Coded R4+DK

Oct 24	Dornier 215	*Destroyed*	From 3/Aufkl.Gr.Ob.d.L. Crashed near St Neots. Shared with Sgt Hogg & PO Fajtl Coded L2+KS
Oct 28	Dornier 17 Z-2	Damaged	Over the North Sea. Shared with Sgt Bartlett.
Oct 28	Dornier 215	Damaged	
Oct 30	Messerschmitt bf 109E-4	Probable	Originally claimed and credited as destroyed but this is now in doubt.
Nov 17	Messerschmitt bf 110 D-3	Damaged	Claimed as Italian BR20. However, it was an Me110 of I/EG210 which crashed in sea off Aldeburgh. Coded S9+MH

APPENDIX C

Pilot Roster 17 Squadron RAF, Battle of Britain July 1 to October 31 1940

Name	*Rank*	*Nationality*	*Remarks*
Bartlett L H	Sgt	British	Joined July 15. Later Group Captain. Awarded DSO.
Bayne A W A	FL	British	Later Squadron Leader DFC. Killed.
Bennette G R	FO	British	Killed in Action August 19, 1942.
Bird-Wilson H A C	PO	British	Later Air Commodore DSO DFC AFC
Blatchford H P	FO	Canadian	Joined Sept 30, to 257 Sdn Oct 1940. DFC Killed in action 1942.
Brett C P N	FO	British	July 12 to August 18.
Britton H W A	PO	British	Killed August 6, 1940
Bumstead R F	Sgt	British	To 111 Sdn August 27. Later commissioned. Awarded DFC.
Cameron N	Sgt	British	Joined October. Later Air Vice Marshal DSO DFC.
Chelmecki M	PO	Polish	Joined September 9. Later Squadron Leader.
Chew C A	Sgt	British	Joined July 15. Later commissioned & awarded AFC. Killed.
Cooke W E	SL	British	Joined August 20. Later killed.
Czernin M B	FO	British	Later Squadron Leader DSO MC DFC.
Dawbarn P L	PO	British	Joined July.
Etherington W J	Sgt	British	Joined July
Fajtl F	FL	Czech	Joined September 25. Later Wing Commander DFC. PoW May 5, 1942 (escaped).
Fopp D	Sgt	Aust	Wounded September 3. Later Squadron Leader, Awarded AFC.
Griffiths G	Sgt	British	Later commissioned. Awarded DFM.
Hanson D H W	FO	British	Killed in Action September 3.
Harper W J	FL	British	Wounded in action.

Hogg R D	Sgt	British	Joined September 11, killed November 11.
Kordula F	PO	Czech	Joined September 25
Kumiega T L	PO	Polish	Joined September 1. Later Squadron Leader.
Leary D C	PO	British	DFC. Killed December 28, 1940
Lines A P	FO	British	July 9 to August 21
MacDougall R I G	SL	British	Left July 18.
Manger K	FO	British	DFC. Killed in action August 11.
Miller A G	SL	British	DFC. Joined August 29.
Morrison J	Sgt	British	Joined August.
Niemiec P	FO	Polish	Joined September 1. Later Squadron Leader
North-Bomford D J	Sgt	British	To 111 Sdn August 28
Palliser C C	Sgt	British	Joined August. Commissioned & DFC, 1944.
Pittman G E	PO	British	
Ross J K	PO	British	DFC. Killed 1942.
Sewell D A	Sgt	British	Later killed.
Soloman N D	PO	British	Joined August 15, killed in action on August 18.
Stevens L W	FO	British	Later killed.
Toyne W A	FL	British	Left July 4. Later Group Captain DFC.
Williams C W	SL	British	Joined July 18. Killed in action on August 25.
Wissler D H	PO	British	Killed in action November 11, 1940.

APPENDIX D

Aeroplanes flown by Manfred Czernin

Avro 621 Tutor	6 FTS	K3390	Flt Cdr's test July 12, 1935
	Netheravon	K3391	First flight May 14, 1935
	1935	K3392	Cross Country July 31, 1935
	A Flight	K3434	First solo May 28, 1935
		K4808	
		K4817	
		K4818	
Hawker Hart	6 FTS	K3759	Solo on type November 1, 1935
(Trainer)	Netheravon	K4945	First on type October 21, 1935
	1935-36	K4947	Flt Cdr's test December 3, 1935
	D Flight	K4949	
		K4951	
		K4953	
		K4955	
Hawker Audax	6 FTS	K4393	First on type February 12, 1936
	Netheravon		
	1935-36		
	D Flight		
Hawker Hart I	57 Sqdn	K1426	Flt Cdr's test February 28, 1936
	Upper Heyford	K2458	
	1936		
	B Flight		
Hawker Hart	83 Sqdn	K3750	December 7, 1936
(Trainer)	Turnhouse		
	1936-37		
	B Flight		
Hawker Hind		K5527	First on type December 7, 1936
		K5528	
		K5529	
		K6634	
		K6635	Height test June 2, 1937. 20,000 ft
		K6636	Royal Escort July 28, 1937
		K6637	
		K6638	Leuchars practice camp, March 1937.

Hawker Hind		K6639 K6640 K6754	
Avro 621 Tutor	83 Sdn Turnhouse 1936-37 B Flight	K3456	Test, April 6, 1937
Blackburn B2	No. 5 ERFTS Hanworth 1938	G-ADFO G-ADFP G-ADFR G-ADFS G-ADFT G-AEBJ G-AEVJ	 First on type June 20, 1938 First solo June 21, 1938
Hawker Hart	No. 5 ERFTS Hanworth 1938	K4432 K4438 K6486 K6529	Standard model Standard model Trainer Trainer
Hawker Audax	No. 5 ERFTS Hanworth 1938	K7439 K8334	
Blackburn B2	No. 5 ERFTS Hanworth 1939 Instructors Course	G-ACEO G-ACRA G-ADFP G-ADFR G-ADFV G-ADLF G-ADZN G-AEBJ G-AEBK	
Hawker Hart (Trainer)	No. 5 ERFTS Hanworth 1939 Instructors Course	K6529 K6530	Last peacetime flight September 1.
Miles M.14A Magister I	No 4 AOS West Freugh 1939	P2403	First on type September 8, 1939
Hawker Henley	No 4 AOS West Freugh 1939	L3296	First on type September 9, 1939
Avro 652A Anson I	No. 1 Ferry Pool, Hucknall, 1939	N1338 N4917 N5303 N5371 N9546	 First on type September 23, 1939
DeHavilland	No. 1 Ferry	N9264	First on type September 25, 1939

Tiger Moth	Pool, Hucknall, 1939		
DeHavilland 82B Queen Bee	No. 1 Ferry Pool, Hucknall, 1939	P4703	First on type September 30, 1939
Fairey Battle	No. 1 Ferry, Pool, Hucknall, 1939	P2360 P5228 P5231 P5292 P6498 P6527 P6533	 First on type September 24, 1939
Hawker Hart (Trainer)	No. 1 Ferry Pool, Hucknall, 1939	K4422 K5880	
Hawker Hind	No. 1 Ferry Pool, Hucknall, 1939	K6843	
Fairey Swordfish	No. 1 Ferry Pool, Hucknall, 1939		
Blackburn Skua	No. 1 Ferry Pool, Hucknall, 1939	L2993 L3039	
Blackburn Roc	No. 1 Ferry Pool, Hucknall, 1939	L3105	
Hawker Demon	No. 1 Ferry Pool, Hucknall, 1939	K5693	
Hawker Hector	No. 1 Ferry Pool, Hucknall, 1939	K9717	
Gloster Gladiator	12 Group Fighter Pool Aston Down 1939-40	K7944 K7945 K7970 K8001 K8016 K8052	
North American Harvard I	12 Group Fighter Pool	P5862	

Harvard I	Aston Down 1939-40		
Hawker Hurricane I	504 Sqdn Debden, 1940		
Hawker	213 Sqdn	N2489	VHF test, April 26, 1940
Hurricane I	Wittering,	N2541	
	1940.	N2551	Air Firing, April 11, 12 & 13, 1940
	A Flight.	N2661	
Hawker Hurricane I	85 Sqdn France, 1940		Destroyed four German aircraft in May 1940, plus one unconfirmed.
Hawker Hurricane I	17 Sqdn France 1940. A Flight		Aircraft coded YB-K, destroyed one He111, June 6, 1940.
Hawker	17 Sqdn	N2666	
Hurricane I	Debden, Tangmere,	P3539	Coded YB-I. Damaged Ju88, July 24.
	Martlesham Heath,	P3673	Coded YB-F. Destroyed Do17, July 12.
	1940.	P3760	Coded YB-H.
	A Flight	P3892	Coded YB-I. Damaged Ju88, August 8.
		V7408	Coded YB-F Manfred's usual a/c. Damaged Me109, August 18. Destroyed Ju88, August 21. Destroyed 3 Me110s, August 25. Destroyed 2 Me110s, September 3. Destroyed Me109, September 5. Destroyed He111, September 5. Probable He111, September 5. Destroyed Me110, September 11. Probable Me109, September 24. Destroyed Me110, September 27 Damaged Do17, October 14. Destroyed Do215, October 24. Damaged Do17, October 28.
		V6553	Coded YB-J. Probable Me109, October 30
		V7500	Coded YB-D. Damaged Me110, November 17, then shot down by Adolf Galland.
		P2972	Damaged Me109, October 27, 1940.

Miles M14A Magister.	17 Sqdn Debden, Tangmere, Martlesham Heath, 1940. A Flight	P6352	Flown November 3, 1940 and May 10, 1941.
Hawker Hurricane I	17 Sqdn Debden, Tangmere, Martlesham Heath, 1941, A Flight	V7408	Coded YB-F. Damaged by Ju88, February 2, 1941.
		P2859	Coded YB-M.
		P2860	Coded YB-J.
		R4078	Coded YB-C.
Hawker Hurricane II	17 Sqdn Debden, Tangmere, Martlesham Heath, 1941. A Flight	Z2571	Coded YB-F. First flight on type February 21. Attacked by Me109s, March 25, 1941.
Hawker Hurricane I	No. 52 OTU Debden & Aston Down, 1941. A Sqdn.	V6605	
		V6666	
		V6743	
		V6942	
		V7425	
		V7746	
		W9115	
		W9175	
Hawker Hurricane II	No. 52 OTU Debden & Aston Down, 1941. A Sqdn.	Z2685	
		Z3397	
		Z3788	
Miles M.9A Master I	No. 52 OTU Debden & Aston Down, 1941. A Sqdn.	N7504	
		N7608	
		N7933	
		N7957	
		N8750	
		N8764	First on type June 5, 1941.
		T8495	
		AZ281	
		AZ317	
		AZ363	
Miles M.14A Magister	No. 52 OTU Debden & Aston Down, 1941. A Sqdn.		
Supermarine	No. 52 OTU	R6632	

Spitfire I	Debden & Aston Down, 1941. A Sqdn.	X4319	First flight on type July 29, 1941.
Supermarine Spitfire V	No. 52 OTU Debden & Aston Down, 1941. A Sqdn.	R6911 AB236	First on type November 11, 1941
Supermarine Spitfire Vb	65 Sqdn Tangmere, 1941	AD411	Coded YT-D. Beat up over Calais December 19.
Supermarine Spitfire Vb	222 Sqdn North Weald, 1941-42	W3207	Coded ZD-F. Minesweeper patrol December 28, 1941.
Supermarine Spitfire Vb	41 Sqdn Tangmere, 1942	BL514	Coded EB-E but changed to EB-F. Flew shipping recce: January 24. Flew sortie over Scharnhorst & Gneisenau February 12, 1942
Curtiss Mohawk IV	146 Sqdn Dinjan & Dum Dum, Assam & India, 1942	BS788	Scramble May 3, 1942
		BS795	First on type, April 5, 1942 Scramble April 5, 1942.
Hawker Audax		K5141	
		K5588	Sector recce: April 10, 1942
	,,	K8335	Recce sortie May 13, 1942
Brewster 339 Buffalo	,,	W8250	Recce sortie April 30 & May 6, 1942 Flew from Dinjan to Dum Dum May 8.
Hawker Hurricane II		BG312	Coded letter 'F' Manfred's usual machine between May & November 1942.
		BE151	Wing formation October 20, 1942
		BE155	Wing formation October 31, 1942
		BM915	Night flying October 23, 1942 Scramble October 24, 1942
Hawker Hurricane II	224 Group, India, 1942-43.		Flew two machines, coded 'D' & 'N'

Manfred Czernin flew nearly 1,060 hours during his flying career. Of the main types he flew the following times:

Hawker Hurricanes	535.25
Hawker Hinds	113.35
Avro Tutors	93.10
Hawker Harts	59.55
Miles Masters	39.25
Supermarine Spitfires	36.50
Blackburn B2s	21.45

APPENDIX E

Squadron Leader Count M. B. Czernin's decorations & medals

DISTINGUISHED SERVICE ORDER

Rewarding individual instances of meritorious or distinguished service in war. Awarded to Commissioned ranks only. Eligible by special mention by name in despatches for "distinguished service under fire, or under conditions equivalent to service in actual combat with the enemy.

MILITARY CROSS

An Army decoration for Commissioned officers in recognition of gallant and distinguished service in action. Also awarded to RAF officers or warrant officers for gallant service on the ground as opposed to flying.

DISTINGUISHED FLYING CROSS

Awarded for an act or acts of valour, courage or devotion to duty, performed whilst flying in active operations against the enemy.

The 1939-45 STAR

Granted for service in operations between September 3, 1939 and August 15, 1945. RAF – To all aircrew who took part in active operations against the enemy subject to the completion of two months in an operational unit.

A bar to the 1939-45 STAR was authorized for the aircrews of Fighter Command in the Battle of Britain between July 1, 1940 to October 31, 1940. This award being denoted by a gilt rose emblem on the ribbon when it alone is worn.

The AIR CREW EUROPE STAR

Awarded for operational flying from the United Kingdom over Europe and including the UK, for a period of two months from September 3, 1939 to June 4, 1944.

The BURMA STAR

Qualifying service in the Burma campaign from December 11, 1941.

The ITALY STAR

Awarded for operational service in Sicily, Italy etc, from June 11, 1943 to May 8, 1945.

The WAR MEDAL 1939-45

Qualification being 28 days service on operational or non-operational service or duties between September 3, 1939 to September 2, 1945.

Mention in Despatches. Denotes by a bronze oak leaf emblem on the War Medal 1939-45.

DEFENCE MEDAL

For three years service at home in areas subjected to air attack between September 3, 1939 to May 8, 1945.

VOLONTARI DELLA LIBERTA

The Italian Volunteers for Liberty medal, awarded to Manfred on September 30, 1945.

The medal was instigated May, 1945 although the actual medal had not been struck up until 1954. Awarded to patriots who volunteered for active service against the enemy and the fascists, 1943-45.

APPENDIX F
(i)

Manfred Czernin's Citations

Award promulgated in the London Gazette October 1, 1940.

DISTINGUISHED FLYING CROSS

Flying Officer Count Manfred Beckett Czernin

(37148) Royal Air Force

This officer has displayed great keenness in his desire to engage the enemy, and has destroyed nine of their aircraft. In August 1940, he led his section in a head-on attack on large formations of enemy aircraft, destroying three of them.

APPENDIX F
(ii)

Award promulgated in the London Gazette December 1, 1944

MILITARY CROSS

Squadron Leader Count Manfred Czernin DFC

(37148)

On the night of 12th–13th June 1944, Squadron Leader Czernin and his W/T Operator were to be dropped into enemy-occupied territory but the reception signals were not satisfactory and they returned to base. On the following night, the reception was again incorrect. Entirely regardless of his own safety, Squadron Leader Count Czernin decided to jump with a view to making a personal reconnaissance of the situation. This he did without arms of any description and with the full knowledge that the Germans are constantly arranging bogus receptions for the receipt of Allied personnel and stores. On landing, he found the reception committee to be friendly. Thereupon he flashed a signal to the aircraft which dropped the W/T Operator and equipment. But for this courageous action, a most vital operation would have had to be postponed at a stage when time is of the utmost importance to the success of the major plan.

APPENDIX F
(iii)

Award promulgated in the London Gazette November 2, 1945.

DISTINGUISHED SERVICE ORDER

Squadron Leader Count Manfred Beckett Czernin MC DFC

(37148) Royal Air Force

Squadron Leader Czernin was parachuted behind the enemy lines in N.W. Italy on 21st March 1945. His task was to co-ordinate the various scattered Partisan units into a unified command and with these forces, to carry out the directions of 15 Army Group. In order to reach his area of operation in the Bergamasco district he had to cross the 9,000 ft Passo del Diaviolo which was completely covered with snow six feet deep. He made two attempts to cross the pass but without success. At 4 am on 4th April he made a further effort and after marching continuously for 24 hours, suffering severely from cold, frost bite and lack of food, he succeeded in crossing the pass. Squadron Leader Czernin immediately commenced to organise the various partisan forces and by his energy and personality quickly built up a large aggressive Partisan Command. This force, under his direction, went into action on 28th April 1945. He secured the unconditional surrender of three of the enemy garrisons whilst other forces under his command eliminated or captured the garrisons of three other places. Later the same day after the whole area had been cleared of the enemy he, with the Partisan Leader, drove into Bergamo in a car draped with the Union Jack to demand the unconditional surrender of the German Forces. The Germans opened fire and Squadron Leader Czernin was forced to withdraw. He then ordered the Partisans to attack the city and arranged for the underground elements in Bergamo to rise simultaneously. At 7 am on 28th April 1945, Squadron Leader Czernin obtained an unconditional surrender from the German General. Throughout his period in the field Squadron Leader Czernin displayed the highest qualities of leadership and by his courage and daring made a notable contribution to the Allied success in North Italy.

Index

* * *

Military Units

Axis Army Units

British Army Units

US Army Units

German Luftwaffe Squadrons & Units

Axis Aeroplanes